The Hidden Room

COLLECTED POEMS, VOLUME ONE

The Hidden Room

COLLECTED POEMS, VOLUME ONE

P. K. Page

The Porcupine's Quill

CANADIAN CATALOGUING IN PUBLICATION DATA

Page, P. K. (Patricia Kathleen), 1916 -
The hidden room : collected poems

Includes index.
ISBN 0-88984-190-X (V. I)   ISBN 0-88984-193-4 (V. 2)

I. Title.

PS8531.A34A17 1997   C811'.54   C97-931632-4
PR9199.3.P3A17 1997

Published by The Porcupine's Quill, 68 Main Street, Erin, Ontario
NOB ITO. Readied for the press by Stan Dragland. Copy edited by
Doris Cowan. Typeset in Galliard, printed on Zephyr Antique laid,
and bound at The Porcupine's Quill Inc.

The cover is after a painting by the author (under the name of P. K.
Irwin). All interior drawings are also by the author.

Represented in Canada by the Literary Press Group. Trade orders
are available from General Distribution Services.

We acknowledge the support of the Canada Council for the Arts
for our publishing programme. The support of the Ontario Arts
Council and the Department of Canadian Heritage through the
Book and Periodical Industry Development Programme is also
gratefully acknowledged.

3   4   •   99   98   97

❧ Acknowledgments

My thanks to Stan Dragland, an inspired editor, who tackled material spanning sixty years and threaded it together in a manner uniquely his own; to Théa Gray who helped me sort through a mass of manuscript and acted as a third eye throughout; to my husband, Arthur Irwin, editor *extraordinaire*; to the late Alan Crawley; to Margaret Atwood, Richard Teleky, Jan Zwicky, Ann Pollock and Jay Ruzesky; and to Arlene Lampert, Constance Rooke and Rosemary Sullivan for thirty years of support.

Acknowledgments are due to the CBC, the Ryerson Press, McClelland & Stewart, the House of Anansi, Oxford University Press, and Brick Books; also to *Preview, Contemporary Verse, First Statement, Northern Review, The Canadian Forum, Poetry: A Magazine of Verse, Saturday Night, The Canadian Poetry Magazine, Tamarack Review, Prism International, Queen's Quarterly, Poetry Australia, The Observer, Encounter, Malahat Review, West Coast Review, here and now, Is., White Pelican, Vancouver Island Poems, Tuatara, Prairie Schooner, Canadian Literature, CVII, Reading, Ariel, The Ontario Review, Vancouver Island Poems, Blackfish, Outposts, Alphabet, Canadian Bookman,* and *Poetry Canada Review.*

To All My Family
and Beyond

❀ Contents

Generation

Melanie's Nite-Book

Evening Dance of the Grey Flies

❈ The Hidden Room

I have been coming here since I was born
never at my will
only when it permits me

Like the Bodleian like the Web
like Borges' aleph
it embodies all

It is in a house
deeply hidden in my head
It is mine and notmine

yet if I seek it
it recedes
down corridors of ether

Each single version
is like and unlike
all the others

a hidden place
in cellar or attic
matrix of evil and good

a room
disguised as a non-room
a secret space

I am showing it to you
fearful you may not
guess its importance

that you will see only
a lumber room
a child's bolt-hole

Will not know it as prism
a magic square
the number nine

To Begin Before I Was Born

❊ *Emergence*

Come before rain;
rise like a dark blue whale
in the pale blue taffeta sea;
lie like a bar in the eyes where the sky should be.
Come before rain.

❀ *The Crow*

By the wave rising, by the wave breaking
high to low;
by the wave riding the air, sweeping the high air low
in a white foam, in a suds,
there
like a churchwarden, like a stiff
turn-the-eye-inward old man
in a cutaway, in the mist
stands
the crow.

❀ *The Mole*

The mole goes down the slow dark personal passage –
a haberdasher's sample of wet velvet moving
on fine feet through an earth that only
the gardener and the excavator know.

The mole is a specialist and truly
opens his own doors; digs as he needs them
his tubular alleyways; and all his hills
are mountains left behind him.

❈ Ecce Homo

London had time to idle in galleries then.

We went together to the gallery in Leicester Square,
Epstein was showing there.
On the way you said
'Polygamy should be legalized ... monogamy is dead.'
A wind of birds interrupted your words.
'Talking of birds,' you said,
'we tarred and feathered his Rima.
No ... not I ... but my race.
We are a queer people,
inarticulate and yet ...
Ah! here is the place.'

We entered the gallery
but what I remember most
was my unexpected entry
into the door of my mind
with Rima as my host,
saying, as you had said,
'Monogamy is dead.'

People had never spoken like that before.
It had always been,
'Lovely weather we're having.'
Or, at the most,
'I wish I hadn't read
that awful book by Cronin, it's obscene.
Hatter's Castle it's called ...
I shouldn't read it.'
Never dreaming a swift awakening was what I needed.

We entered the little room where *Ecce Homo* stood,
but it was bare to me.

I was away with Rima, discussing polygamy.
And then I felt your hand
tighten upon my arm
and heard you say in alarm,
'To understand,
Christ must be forgotten.
this is the mighty God. The God begotten
straight from the minds of the prophets,
straight from their fearful minds.
This is the God of plagues,
not the Christ who died
for love of humanity – the beautiful gentle Boy,
humorous, sunny-eyed.
Before you look,' you said,
'remember, remember it is not Christ,' you said.

I looked and the little room was filled with might,
with the might of fear in stone,
immense and shackled.
The flesh that covered the bone
seemed bone itself,
terrible, holy … you could not take a breath –
the Man, deformed, thick-hipped,
the God of Death,
in a little room in a gallery in Leicester Square,
silently standing there.

'There is much we do not know,'
you turned to me.
(Behold the Man, Rima, polygamy!)
'I think we should find somewhere nice and quiet for tea.
To think,' you said.
I nodded my head. 'To think,' I said.
And like a young tree I put out a timid shoot
and prayed for the day, the wonderful day when it bore its fruit.
And suddenly we were out in the air again.

London had time to idle in galleries then.

❋ *The Clock of Your Pulse*

Tell the time by the face of the passer-by –
the dial of flesh bounded by minutes and touched by hands –
where the treat of time ticks out its dividends –
an hour or nothing – alone as a hawker's cry.

Mark time telescoped to an inch that was once a mile,
and space stretched out to a mile that was once an inch;
hear nothing, then the anonymous foot's crunch,
nothing again; the whole a faded photograph of a smile.

Mark time like a year, registered in an hour,
space Lilliputian, streets too small for the feet,
unhurried history occur in the 'now' and the great
body fold like a blade to slip through the door.

Refer to the clock of your pulse as an arbiter,
hear it tick like a gong in your ear, by a madman beaten,
hear it switch and click sharp as a dark death beetle,
explode like a depth charge, shrill like a howitzer.

Know nothing sure; expand and shrink without warning,
know neither the size of a room nor the height of a tree;
the street like a land contracts to a map as you go,
there is no certain length of time between evening and morning.

Plug in the electrical clock and observe it play
with pattern of minutes, hearing its regular chime –
a practical joker keeping its personal time,
or a child that plays with its hands through the nebulous day.

Stop on the stumble of stairs where the grandfather clock
stands like an upright coffin and counts the dead
with the backwards and forwards swing of its corpse's leg;
when the stairs are a beanstalk you are a bloodless Jack.

Let the clocks run down, let them point to noon or midnight,
while the stippled pulse of your wrist is the guest of honour
and taps like a pad of flesh or fires like a gunner
at the moving target of space with a false gunsight.

❀ Desiring Only

Desiring only the lean sides of the stomach
sagging towards each other, unupholstered ...
pass me nothing of love done up in chocolates
or the fat first fruits of the tree
you planted from seed.

Desiring only the bone on the Mount of Venus
and the death rattle caught in the musical powder box ...
pass me no hand, then, as offertory,
no, nor sound of your voice.
Keep silent and do not touch me.
Even the air on my face is an effrontery.

Desiring only the bare soles of the feet
pacing triumphantly the ultimate basement ...
pass me no thick-carpeted personal contact,
nor little slippers of pity and understanding.

❁ The Understatement

I speak not in hyperbole,
I speak in true words muted to their undertone,
choosing a pebble where you would a stone,
projecting pebbles to immensity.

For where love is no word can be compounded
extravagant enough to frame the kiss
and so I use the under-emphasis,
the muted note, the less than purely rounded.

❀ Remember the Wood

When the face grows cheese-pale and bitter
with the deception of the mood,
heart, remember the wood.

Dark it is and interlaced
with branches forcing back the sun;
damp as a fungus still unguessed,
unsweet as carrion.

Walking man-high beneath the trees
with trigger-lidded eyes half shut,
the branches are your enemies,
the damp your funeral, but

below the level of those eyes
unfolds the trillium.
A foot could crush the midnight skies:
stamp on the star of Bethlehem.

So when the face grows pale and bitter
with the deception of the mood,
and mind fingers the fallen shutter,
heart, remember the wood.

Before the window the still body
becomes observer; centipede eyes
worry a surface with action and never
see, though they may look forever.
The still body slips gently into
the scene beyond the window;
the still body finds it can hear
sounds that demand a sounding board wider than the ear.

(To be precise about the expanse of flesh
in retrospect is hard
as writing on a calling card
with the blunt thumb dipped in ink.
What body has known
eyes scuttle from
and mind skims over
with the tolerance of the heart for a no-good lover.)

Before the window the still body
dissembles and ultimately forms –
becomes a glass bauble, holding a street scene
some hand has tilted so the snow falls.
(You have seen these baubles in your grandmother's house,
souvenir of a winter in Switzerland?)
Before the window, behind the gramophone,
the snow and Chopin mingle;
the flake-note is a single
unit, a fusion moving, moving behind the bone.

Flake notes sweep downward, idle,
rest on the air in groups;
move up; describe a circle;
split, dangle, slip in streaks.
The storm becomes two notes sounding over and over –
two flakes that saunter, race and overtake each other.

Down the tubular trunks of trees
snow grains slide like rice –
flow down dark transparent shoots
entering earth through the trees' roots.
Twigs and boughs of trees
suddenly growing downward
guide white kernels groundward.

The wall's smooth weight of brick
is strictly pointillistic –
white paint flecks
the red bricks
and passes through the absorbent wall.
Air that was empty now is full –
an earthbound cloud,
a wide blowing sheet, a tight wrapping shroud,
moulding the skeleton.

Is this death? Is death a swirling
flake-note ballet? A white
flag flying against the night
body has borrowed; a whirling army
invading darkness? A still body?

Hinges whine and a door opens.
'What are you thinking of?'
'Snow,' I say. With the word spoken
the bauble is broken.
Flesh contracts and ear and eye
splinter the flake-note –
snow is snow and Chopin Chopin
recorded singly – eye and ear
watching there, and listening here.
'Thinking of snow?'
'Thinking of snow.'

❀ *Death*

So this was death –
the hummingbird's soft throat
bound in a dark and crimson coat
of blood.
This flood
of feeling in her heart
was the essential part
of life.
The strife
of living was a little thing beside
the sobbing, throbbing eventide
of breath.

❀ *For G.E.R.*

Neither the trailing and lifting of the remembered hand through water
nor the paling or flushing of the remembered skin
is as permanent with pain as footsteps in wet mortar
or winter settling in.

For the thought of the living image evades the eye
as quicksilver clutched, or the empty colour of wind;
and the remembered voice is soft with sound as a cloud across the sky.

The quicksilver splits and beads and the beads are shaken;
The wind dies out in a rattle among the trees,
and the cloud is blown and even the sky forsaken.

But the remembered voice, the remembered skin, the hand,
is sunlight only, or loveliness defined
in a young rain over a sun-baked land
or a visionary mind.

✺ *As on a Dark Charger*

As on a dark charger
the night wind arrives,
brushing the thick, cold laurel leaves
and the slim willow knives.
    The night is opulent, larger
    to greet the young wind
    riding his dark charger.
But the wild swallows
and martins are pinned
like paper copies of birds
to the protecting eaves
above the slim willow knives
and laurel leaves.
    As, on a dark charger,
    insolent, rich,
    rides the young wind
    over the land.
    A new-peeled switch
    in his bare hand.
    Onward he swings,
    grows larger and larger,
    whistles and sings
    as on a dark charger.

Night Garden

❀ *Journey*

Never resist the going train of the dream
risen and steaming on hard tracks
through Breughel landscape
or troubled slum.

The houses and the faces fabricate
heart's drop to terror and eyes' flight to madness;
cling, madam, to the blunt caboose like a streamer
or prod the engine.

Oh, do not lag behind syringe of whistle
douching your ears; on spongy fingers
number the revs. per min.
They are your tempo.

You may be boxcar baggage or begonia,
porter with epaulettes and moon for navel;
the way is watercolour to the station,
the stop is limbo.

❋ *Round Trip*

The passenger boards the waiting train –
he is white
and poised as the sculptured gull in flight;
his matching bags might be packed with air –
they are neat and flat.
Now he removes his hat,
smooths back his hair,
arranges his long pressed legs away from the aisle.
(The girl inside, meanwhile,
afraid of adventure,
trembles against his wrought-iron ribs like paper.)
He waves through the window a last farewell,
his pale
sigh of a hand caressing the delicate pane
blots out the faces one by one as though
he were snuffing candle flames.

All is prepared for the incredible journey:
in the baggage car his trunks contain a sword,
binoculars and compass, powdered food,
shorts and a solar topee for the south,
letters of introduction and a mask.
A lifetime lies behind him
he has left
the tightly frozen rivers of his blood
the plateaux of his boredom
and the bare
buttonholes his pallid eyes had cut.

> Ahead – perhaps the mountains and the hot
> colours of the tropics
> and the sun
> awaiting only his miraculous foot.

Settled, he sighs. The train devours its track
(the girl cries for her mother),
he is hot,
adjusts the air conditioner,
dares not
shed his respectable beginner's coat
fearing the ill-drawn map it might uncover.
Suffers unspeaking,
neither nods nor smiles
to anyone nearby.
Decides the country he is passing through
may offer some escape,
straightens his tie
and contemplates the view.

Unveiling the sluggish eye that is drugged with future
he notes the place where the sienna soil
makes an incision in the field of mustard
clotted against the acid drops of the poplars;
dilates the pupil's I as he approaches
the perpetual great-god-green upending marshes
where grey and ageing barns with a family likeness
are scattered about like relatives in a village.
A bridge against the sky,
with metal girders
that droop in long black leaves,
forms a grove of palms –
a hot illusion set with circling birds.

But 'like' or 'as' is not what he is searching.
Something is hidden in the scenery still –
the hero hovers just behind the curtain
articulating the perfect unheard words
and the changing country is only a view that swings
the silent globes of the eyes but nothing more,
for his eyes, unlike a doll's, have no lead ball
attached behind the nose to rise and fall.

A white house, stark with the memory of home,
jumps from the unseen field – an ace in his face –
and slips back swiftly in the indolent pack.
(He feels the girl's long-fingered hands like tears,
feels the contortions of her weeping face.)
And his mind in a tantrum draws its filmy shutter
invisibly across the dot of sight
turning the country into the negative, no
country of faint or fit.
Trees pass and pass,
the quick rush of their noise
the Niagara of blood evacuating the head,
while passengers in a trance of boredom or bright
with the coloured excitement of a child in fever
move along the corridors of plush
as if they had no choice.
A surgeon's voice pierces his deafened ears:
'Trains don't take you anywhere, nor cars –
they're just another standstill thing on wheels
screaming at full-speed stop through the moving landscape
and returning you to yourself –
it's a boomerang business
with the pretty revolving set of the old-time movies.'

The traveller sleeps,
in dreams explores the place
where everything is foreign:
the orange groves and the quick
walk of the women
which fit together like glass arithmetic.
The sheen that lies on gutters in gold leaf.
(The dream of falling followed him, he fell
sideways along sierras
down through boughs
where monkeys smiled at him with his own mouth.)
But everyone recognized him for their own.
In such sweet rain his ears and armpits grew
flowers and hummingbirds were part of him –

hanging jewels upon lapel and hat.
At night the oranges and lemons cut
small amber caves from darkness where he sat
and the mercurial rivers found their seas
at any spot he bathed.
When storms came up, fish glanced the thickened air.
Nothing was permanent and everywhere
immediate as music, slick as silk.
With daylight silver girls on silver stilts
called in his turret window as he woke.
(But still the dream of falling followed him:
he fell through bubble faces, fell through trees,
he fell through purple fulminating smoke,
through hands that were only gloves and arms that were sleeves.)
Then falling passed and everywhere he looked
was bright, for diamonds had replaced his eyes.

Awake he sees the baking soil, the cracked
packets of earth
where thin anaemic weeds are grass snakes.
Following that, the desert:
sand seeps between the badly fitting windows,
clings to his teeth,
settles beneath his nails.
Later he feels it pumping through his heart –
a mechanical hourglass.
Invisible as lice it crawls and spreads
over the sheets, the pillow's stuffed with it
and all night long it roars in his ears,
sifts over him as if it is wanted and loved,
settles in crease and pore; is his.
To be caught in a glacier, he thinks, to be mint
in the heart of an ice cube,
to be contained in anything smooth, to touch
a hardwood floor in Iceland.
(The girl inside, with a rosary of sand
repeats her Aves and the Paternoster.)
He dozes fitfully and dreams he wakes,

wakes, thinks he's dreaming, tries to break his dreams,
feels feverish, attempts to take his pulse.

Light settles on his face at last in mist,
raising the blind the world is mist forever
and focus has to shift and shift for far
and near are now identical –
colourless, shapeless – echoing ghosts of snow.
Oh, where is what he dreamed, forever where
the landscape for his pattern? The desired
and legendary country he had planned?
In all this mist, he says, in all this mist,
a man might not exist,
a man might be
an empty snakeskin.
And as he thinks, the train is losing speed,
behaves as if the mist had clogged its wheels,
becomes a caterpillar mired in glue
                                    and stops.
'Home Town,' the porter calls. 'End of the track.'
And all the passengers, as if they knew,
and undeceived by fantasy or folder,
descend the waiting steps
and vanish in the mist
which hides the station and obstructs the view.

The traveller is lost. (His crying girl
grown into empress
moans, 'Betrayed! Betrayed!')
He blocks his ears to her,
smooths back his hair,
prepares for the adventure with a smile,
swings to the door with an explorer's stride
and steps upon the platform to be met
by everyone he left.
Their waving hands are little flags for him
fluttering and blowing. Coming near
he hears the words their moving mouths repeat:

that nothing's changed, that everything's the same.
And though he cannot see because of mist
he know's it's true – that everything's the same.

Forever, everywhere, for him, the same.

And though all this was nowhere there were planes
above that flew upon a course
and drew our eyes to them;
some, swooping low, sailed over our flat faces
and gave us sound, like a present;
in some we saw the daring pilots' profiles
different from ours.
It was a tense and visionary moment when they came
for those of us who did not sleep or run
back to the womb.
Some of us danced
and held up flowers and once
a small boy with a catapult propelled
a paper round a pebble straight
into the open cockpit saying, 'Land.'

Lately they must have found a shorter route
from where they started from to where they went
and now the skies are a disappointment, more
endless and open like ourselves. But one
among us thought the problem out,
declares we are to follow; from above
the certainty of east and west will come.
He climbed upon a gable, cried, 'From here
I see beyond the limit of my nose,'
and clambered down again. Already he
has built the body of a plane –
oh, slight
with perilous, delicate ribs and a great space
where it seems to call for wings.
He has been denied
the public help and sanction
but there are those
who work with him day and night.

In the past we had only dreamed of learning the key,
of the compass discovered,
the needle pointing to us –
and later, waking up,
had found geography and history merged –
two figures beautifully entwined,
who withdrew as we approached
and left us behind.
But now,
the knowledge imminent, we must
stand close and touch each other,
lean upon
each other's shoulders gently.
When it comes
I think it will come violently –
a bolt
of lightning lighting for us more
than we have seen before –
and weld us, if we touch,
firmly as one,
oh, finally, as us.

Where the bog ends, there, where the ground lips, lovely
is love, not lonely.
                        Land is
love, round with it, where the hand is;
wide with love, cleared scrubland, grain
on a coin.
Oh, the wheatfield, the rock-bound rubble;
the untouched hills
                        as a thigh smooth;
the meadow.
Not only the poor soil lovely, the outworn prairie,
but the green upspringing,
the lark-land,
the promontory.

A lung-born land,
a breath spilling,
scanned by the valvular heart's
field glasses.

Certainly there had been nothing but the extraordinary rain for a long
    time,
nothing but the rain, the grey buildings, the grey snow,
when landscape broke the lens and smacked his face
with a flag of blue
and the white thunder of snow
rolling the hills.

Hurry was in his veins,
violence vaulted the loose-box of his head
where the old cantankerous horse was harsh with its hooves
and hurry was hot in the straw
and snapped in the eyes
of the innocent traveller.

And flex and flux were there
like acrobats
waving their banners.
So declamatory was his blood
that he owned the train:
its whistle was in his throat,
its wheels in his brain.

Once he became a panoramic view.
The white of the valleys and hills
his own still flesh
outstretched and magnified;
the single house, with lights too early lit,
the incredible carton of his shining head.

But speed had robbed him,
he was forced to change
his contours and his outlook and his range.

Riding through forest it was dark again
and the great coniferous branches brushed his face
and the snow, packed round the multiple trunks, was dead.

Rabbit spoor resembled his memory
of what he once had been –
faint against faintness, definite as dust,
of the no-taste of wafers, of the warmth
that neither gives nor takes.
Past was a pastel rubbed as he hurried past.

And now that the tunnel of trees was done, his eyes
sprinted the plain where house lights in the dusk
fired pistols for the race that led him on.
He shed the train like a snake its skin, he dodged
the waiting cameras which with a simple click
could hold him fast to the spot beside the track.
And as the air came into his lungs he stood
there in the dark at his destination, knowing
somewhere – to left? to right? – he was walking home
and his shoulders were light and white as though wings were growing.

❀ *Images of Angels*

Imagine them as they were first conceived:
part musical instrument and part daisy
in a white manshape.
Imagine a crowd on the Elysian grass
playing ring-around-a-rosy,
mute except for their singing,
their gold smiles
gold sickle moons in the white sky of their faces.
Sex, neither male nor female,
name and race, in each case, simply angel.

Who, because they are white and gold, has made them holy
but never to be loved or petted, never to be friended?

Not children, who imagine them more simply,
see them more coloured and a deal more cosy,
yet somehow mixed with the father, fearful and fully
realized when the vanishing bed
floats in the darkness,
when the shifting point of focus, that drifting star,
has settled in the head.

More easily, perhaps, the little notary
who, given one as a pet, could not
walk the sun-dazzled street
with so lamb-white a companion.
For him its loom-large skeleton –
one less articulated than his own –
would dog his days with doom
until, behind the lethal lock
used for his legal documents
he guiltily shut it up.
His terror then that it escape
and smiling call for him at work.
Less dreadful for his public shame,

• • •   41

worse for his private guilt
if in that metal vault
it should die mute
and in the hour that he picked it up
he found it limp and boneless as a flower.

Perhaps, more certainly perhaps, the financier.
What businessman would buy as he buys stock
as many could cluster on a pin?
Angels are dropping, angels going up.
He could not mouth such phrases and chagrin
would sugar round his lips as he said 'angel'.
For though he mocks their mention he cannot
tie their tinsel image to a tree
without the momentary lowering of his lids
for fear that they exist in worlds which he
uneasy, reconstructs from childhood's memory.

The anthropologist with his tidy science,
had he stumbled upon one unawares,
found as he finds an arrowhead, an angel,
a – what of a thing –
primitive as a daisy
might with his ice-cold eye have assessed it coolly.
But how, despite his detailed observations,
could he face his learned society and explain?
'Gentlemen, it is thought that they are born
with harps and haloes
as the unicorn with its horn.
Study discloses them white and gold as daisies.'

Perhaps only a dog could accept them wholly,
be happy to follow at their heels
and bark and romp with them in the green fields.

Or, take the nudes of Lawrence and impose
asexuality upon them; those
could meet with ease these gilded albinos.

Or a child, not knowing they were angels, could
wander along an avenue hand in hand
with his new milk-white playmates,
take a step
and all the telephone wires would become taut
as the high strings of a harp
and space be merely the spaces between strings
and the world mute, except for a thin singing,
as if a sphere – big enough to be in it
and yet small
so that a glance through the lashes
would show it whole –
were fashioned very finely out of wire
and turning in a wind.

But say the angelic word
and *this* innocent
with his almost unicorn
would let it go
for even a child would know
that angels should be flying in the sky,
and, feeling implicated in a lie,
his flesh would grow
cold
and snow
would cover the warm and sunny avenue.

❀ Christmas Eve – Market Square

City of Christmas, here, I love your season,
where in the market square,
bristled and furry
like a huge animal
the fir trees lie
silent, awaiting buyers.
    It's as if
    they hold the secrets of a Christmas sealed –
    as statues hold their feelings sealed in stone –
    and burst to bells and baubles on their own
    within the warmth and lightness of a house
    as trees in springtime burst to buds and birds.

The sellers, bunched and bundled,
hold their ears,
blow lazy boas as they call their wares,
and children out of legends pulling sleds,
prop tall trees straight in search of symmetry
and haul the spiky aromatic wonder
of *tree* through a snowy world.
    Almost the tree sings through them in their carols,
    almost grows taller in their torsos, is
    perfectly theirs, as nothing ever was.

The soft snow falls,
vague smiling drunkards weave
gently as angels through a street of feathers;
balancing bulging parcels with their wings
they tip-toe where the furry monster grows
smaller and hoarier
and nerveless sprawls
flat on its mammoth, unimagined face.
    While in far separate houses
    all its nerves
    spring up like rockets,

unknown children see
a miracle
and unknown children cry
to cut the ceiling, not to lop the tree.

❀ *Earthquake*

Look at the sky, she said
as the earth quaked
and others were taking cover.
You might see God
in the brief irregular shape
framed by the falling hotels
with their ferns hurtling.
In the space between
the still standing church
and the teetering Five and Ten
he might be seen
as small and bright as a straight pin
narrowly smiling.
This is the kind of time
He might appear to be near
shining and clear.
Look at the sky, she said,
but brimful brick
filled in a twinkling
the dwindling opening
and sky came tumbling.

❀ Arras

Consider a new habit – classical,
and trees espaliered on the wall like candelabra.
How still upon that lawn our sandalled feet.

But a peacock rattling its rattan tail and screaming
has found a point of entry. Through whose eye
did it insinuate in furled disguise
to shake its jewels and silk upon that grass?

The peaches hang like lanterns. No one joins
those figures on the arras.
                              Who am I
or who am I become that walking here
I am observer, other, Gemini,
starred for a green garden of cinema?

I ask, what did they deal me in this pack?
The cards, all suits, are royal when I look.
My fingers slipping on a monarch's face
twitch and go slack.
I want a hand to clutch, a heart to crack.

No one is moving now, the stillness is
infinite. If I should make a break ...
take to my springy heels ...? But nothing moves.
The spinning world is stuck upon its poles,
the stillness points a bone at me. I fear
the future on this arras.
                              I confess:

It was my eye.
Voluptuous it came.
Its head the ferrule and its lovely tail
folded so sweetly; it was strangely slim
to fit the retina. And then it shook

and was a peacock – living patina,
eye-bright – maculate!
Does no one care?

I thought their hands might hold me if I spoke.
I dreamed the bite of fingers in my flesh,
their poke smashed by an image, but they stand
as if within a treacle, motionless,
folding slow eyes on nothing. While they stare
another line has trolled the encircling air,
another bird assumes its furled disguise.

❀ *Photos of a Salt Mine*

How innocent their lives look,
how like a child's
dream of caves and winter, both combined:
the steep descent to whiteness
and the stope
with its striated walls
their folds all leaning as if pointing to
the greater whiteness still,
that great white bank
with its decisive front,
that seam upon a slope,
salt's lovely ice.

And wonderful underfoot the snow of salt,
the fine
particles a broom could sweep,
one thinks
muckers might make angels in its drifts,
as children do in snow,
lovers in sheets,
lie down and leave imprinted where they lay
a feathered creature holier than they.

And in the outworked stopes
with lamps and ropes
up miniature Matterhorns
the miners climb,
probe with their lights
the ancient folds of rock –
syncline, anticline –
and scoop from darkness an Aladdin's cave:
rubies and opals glitter from its walls.

But hoses douse the brilliance of these jewels,
melt fire to brine.

Salt's bitter water trickles thin and forms
slow fathoms down
a lake within a cave
lacquered with jet –
white's opposite.
There grey on black the boating miners float
to mend the stays and struts of that old stope
and deeply underground
their words resound,
are multiplied by echo, swell and grow
and make a climate of a miner's voice.

So all the photographs like children's wishes
are filled with caves or winter,
innocence
has acted as a filter,
selected only beauty from the mine.
Except in the last picture, shot
from an acute high angle. In a pit
figures the size of pins are strangely lit
and might be dancing but you know they're not.
Like Dante's vision of the nether hell
men struggle with the bright cold fires of salt
locked in the black inferno of the rock:
the filter here, not innocence but guilt.

❈ *The Snowman*

Ancient nomadic snowman has rolled round.
His spoor: a wide swathe on the white ground
signs of a wintry struggle where he stands.

Stands? Yes, he stands. What snowman sat?
Legless, indeed, but more as if he had
legs than had not.

White double O, white nothing nothing, this
the child's first man on a white paper, his
earliest and fistful image is

now three-dimensional. Abstract. Everyman.
Of almost manna, he is still no man
no person, this so personal snowman.

O transient un-inhabitant, I know
no child who, on seeing the leprous thaw
undo your whitened torso and face of snow

would not, had he the magic
call you back
from that invisible attack

even knowing he can, with the new miracle
of another and softer and whiter snowfall
make you again, this time more wonderful.

* * *

Innocent single snowman. Overnight
brings him – a bright
omen – a thunderbolt of white.

But once I saw a mute in every yard
come like a plague; a stock-still multitude
and all stone-buttoned, bun-faced and absurd.

And next day they were still there but each
had changed a little as if all had inched
forward or back, I barely knew which;

and greyed a little too, grown sinister
and disreputable in their sooty fur,
numb, unmoving and nothing moving near.

And as far as I could see the snow was scarred
only with angels' wing marks or the feet of birds
like twigs broken upon the snow or shards

discarded. And I could hear no sound
as far as I could hear except a round
kind of echo without end

rung like a hoop below them and above
jarring the air they had no need of
in a landscape without love.

❀ *Mystics Like Miners*

Mystics like miners wear their lamps
strapped to their palely wandering brows.
Voices disown their gentle mouths,
come loud and crystalline as coal
but cold to shake an alien ear.

Primitive darkness holds their loins,
their long extended wrists and hands
are heavy with whiteness as a bone:
the wish El Greco's charcoal drew,
the shape to fit a candled ghost.

Each holds the shaft within him; it
is light and easy for ascension
yet, rising, he finds flowers too bright
(what saint of painted gold and red,
alive, could really wear those colours?)
and sky so high, so baby blue
a blue-eyed boy alone could bear it.

Descending the familiar shaft
mystics like miners throw their lamps
full on the darkness daily. Probe
symbol for solid, solid for
its simplest symbol. They explore
in wisdom, never innocence.

Those in the vegetable rain retain
an area behind their sprouting eyes
held soft and rounded with the dream of snow
precious and reminiscent as those globes –
souvenir of some never nether land –
which hold their snowstorms circular, complete,
high in a tall and teakwood cabinet.

In countries where the leaves are large as hands
where flowers protrude their fleshy chins
and call their colours
an imaginary snowstorm sometimes falls
among the lilies.
And in the early morning one will waken
to think the glowing linen of his pillow
a northern drift, will find himself mistaken
and lie back weeping.
And there the story shifts from head to head,
of how, in Holland, from their feather beds
hunters arise and part the flakes and go
forth to the frozen lakes in search of swans –
the snow light falling white along their guns,
their breath in plumes.
While tethered in the wind like sleeping gulls
ice boats await the raising of their wings
to skim the electric ice at such a speed
they leap jet strips of naked water,
and how these flying, sailing hunters feel
air in their mouths as terrible as ether.
And on the story runs that even drinks
in that white landscape dare to be no colour;
how, flasked and water clear, the liquor slips
silver against the hunters' moving hips.
And of the swan in death these dreamers tell
of its last flight and how it falls, a plummet,

pierced by the freezing bullet
and how three feathers, loosened by the shot,
descend like snow upon it.
While hunters plunge their fingers in its down
deep as a drift, and dive their hands
up to the neck of the wrist
in that warm metamorphosis of snow
as gentle as the sort that woodsmen know
who, lost in the white circle, fall at last
and dream their way to death.

And stories of this kind are often told
in countries where great flowers bar the roads
with reds and blues which seal the route to snow –
as if, in telling, raconteurs unlock
the colour with its complement and go
through to the area behind the eyes
where silent, unrefractive whiteness lies.

❋ The Age of Ice

The white months come like a floating sail
that sails into the eye
and the coloured pupils fade
as swiftly as if they froze;

and the white days darken at five
like the inside of a kitchen cup
and the bones that pipe the flesh
turn into platinum wire.

This is the north. Its nip
is white, its teeth are nice.
No several summers know its heat
though heat lives in its ice.

Negative as a mule
it takes the nick of time
in its treacherous tight lip
and rubs it to a fur;

prepares a shaggy scene
where nothing bears its shape
surely, but substitutes
another in its place.

Then puts forth flowers and fronds
more delicate than spring
for the deceptive eye
fondly to gaze upon.

Puts on a frosted glass.
The giraffe's neck of the milk
lifts to the long hand
of skeletal lace.

While cut from white paper
by eyes' circumference
the endless snow plains circle
Forever round and round.

And over them the running Will
moves like a dot
but the lazy Wish in a spring melt
slips on no sure foot.

Oh, the world is bright with starch
and perilous blooms are born
precarious on the branch
but their beauty numbs the root

of the pillared I. Between
the Will and the Wish is glass
and the glass is cold between
and the glass is frosting up.

Only fingers can touch
the terrible frozen space
where the hot spray of the Wish
freezes glistening.

The albino Christmas tree
clinks in the inner ear.
The eye is cold and clear.
The splinter seeks the heart.

See, see the figure by the fire
once February has set in
sitting in synthetic heat
beneath an imitation sun.

See, see the layers the body wears
the bandages of wool
binding a dichotomy
now indivisible.

Observe the censored mail
the guardians in the hall
the lock upon the arch
that never swung a door.

Observe the narrow space
as finite as a pin
where nobody goes out
and nobody comes in.

Where wool is well and ill
is nakedness and Will
is woebegone and lost
long since in winter frost.

But look, the tree is traced
with burning buds of ice
with delicate brittle buds
the burning tree is iced.

See how the pane is glazed
with fiddleheads and fronds.
Forerunner of the spring
these urgent ferns.

The spring grows seeds of snow.
First signal of the spring
the trees autumnal red
preceding green.

Retrace the steps: the white
Indian pipes that chilled
as if with ice the quick
warm fingers of the child.

The unexpected frost
that left the catkin charred
the laundered underclothes
like corpses in the yard.

See how each season holds
another in its heart
the two polarities
are never poles apart.

So let your hand become
as naked as the tongue
reach outward through the glass
take winter in your palm.

And feel this age of ice
melt into spring
with the quick sound about
of water running.

❀ *This Cold Man*

Now this cold man in his garden feels the ice
thawing from branches of his lungs and brain;
the blood thins out in artery and vein,
the stiff eyes slip again.

Kneeling in welters of narcissus his
dry creaking joints bend with a dancer's ease,
the roughened skin softens beneath the rain

and all that he had clutched, held tightly locked
behind the fossil frame
dissolves, flows free
in saffron covering the willow tree
and coloured rivers of the rockery.

Yellow and white and purple is his breath,
his hands are curved and cool for cupping petals,
the sharp green shoots emerging from the beds
all whistle for him

until he is the garden – heart the sun
and all his body soil;
glistening jonquils blossom from his skull,
the bright expanse of lawn his stretching thighs
and something rare and perfect, yet unknown,
stirs like a foetus just behind his eyes.

❀ *This Is Another Spring*

There is no mention made of leaf cries,
bird like a ball thrown,
or sea in the city.
I would think instead
of laundry, light on clothespegs
in a ravel of sun;
think of my neighbour-knowledge,
the voice that was a finger
pulling a blind
now is a cough at midnight,
a radio programme.

Where balconies hang
Spring is made ugly with reason,
bird notes chip the air
and let the red brick stand –
promise of summer sulkiness;
the window ledge
will pout for a full season.

The time is Spring
and married men in bowlers
seek a green tunnel
from the patient street;
tasting the tempest of leaves
they wince and lift
dredged ecstasy upon anaemic shoulders.

Oh dead, this, dead;
destruction in the pollen
where winds sew 'private'
on the budding trees
and women's faces are a fusillade
pointed at nothing
fixed behind the flower.

Trick out the hope
in a sprigged cornflower dress,
perform the rope trick
with a silken thread,
lean on the railing
where the rubber pigeon
rocks like a bathtub bird for gravel bread.

❀ *Elegy*

This spring is all small horses and stars
but you have closed your pores to its bombardment,
shut yourself up with the night that flowed into you like ink.

When that black haemorrhage began
your doors opened as if to sunlight
and the darkness roared in like a tidal bore.
Now your least thought is the poor type on cheap newsprint.

What whiteness in you called to be cancelled, pulled
darkness from the two opposing poles
so that you dribble black when you speak
to the accompaniment of muffled drums?

You, white and sewn with scarlet once,
walked giddy with gold
your gilded name grew in our heads and shone
now black is the colour of our true love's name.

First we mourned you as if dead
and covered you with flowers
but when the blackness trickled on our hands
we stepped out of your deadly nightshade.

And if we cry now it is because your green tree
turned too rapidly into coal
and because we have seen our whole hearts
and known them black-edged as mourning envelopes.

And because the stars of this spring will not dazzle our eyes
nor the small white horses accept sugar
lightly with feathered lips from such pied palms.

The Leaning Tower of Self

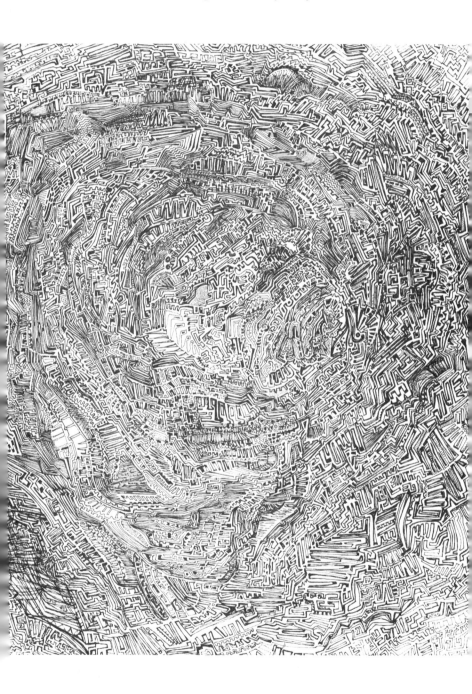

❀ *If It Were You*

If it were you, say, you
who scanning the personal map one day knew
your sharp eyes water and grow colour-blind,
unable to distinguish green from blue
and everything terribly run together as if rain
had smudged the markings on the paper –
a child's painting after a storm –
and the broad avenue erased,
the landmarks gone;
and you, bewildered – not me this time and not
the cold unfriendly neighbour or the face in the news –
who walked a blind circle in a personal place;

and if you became lost, say, on the lawn,
unable to distinguish left from right
and that strange longitude that divides the body
sharply in half – that line that separates
so that one hand could never be the other –
dissolved and both your hands were one,
then in the garden though birds went on with their singing
and on the ground
flowers wrote their signatures in coloured ink –
would you call help like a woman assaulted,
cry to be found?

No ears would understand. Your friends and you
would be practically strangers, there would be no face
more familiar than this unfamiliar place
and there would be walls of air, invisible, holding
you single and directionless in space.

First you would be busy as a woodsman marking
the route out, making false starts and then
remembering yesterday when it was easy
you would grow lazy.

Summer would sit upon you then as on a stone
and you would be
tense for a time beneath the morning sun
but always lonely
and birds perhaps would brush your coat and become
angels of deliverance
for a moment only;
clutching their promising wings you would discover
they were elusive and gone
as the lost lover.
Would you call Ariel, Ariel, in the garden,
in a dream within a dream be Orpheus
and for certain minute take a step
delicately across the grass?

If so, there would be no answer or reply
and not one coming forward from the leaves.
No bird nor beast with a challenging look
or friendly.
Simply nothing but you and the green garden,
you and the garden.

Then there would be the things your head
had prepared for your fingers:
rooting the dandelion from the lawn and training
the runner up the pole
or clipping the privet hedge
and always explaining
your actions by the phrase:
There's work to be done.
And when the garden was complete, the stones
stacked in the rockery
and the trees pruned,
the slugs and the cutworms dead,
your fingers then would signal to your head
wanting a meaning for their continuing movements.
And there would be shoots again to be clipped on the hedge
and weeds entangling the flower beds.

There you might stay forever, mechanically
occupied, but if you raised your head
madness would rush at you from the shrubbery
or the great sun, stampeding through the sky,
would stop and drop –
a football in your hands –
and shrink as you watched it
to a small dark dot
forever escaping focus
like the injury to the cornea which darts
hard as a cinder across the sight but dims
fading into the air like a hocus-pocus
the minute that you are aware
and stare at it.

Might you not, if it were you,
bewildered, broken,
slash your own wrists, commit
an untidy murder in the leafy lane
and scar the delicate air with your cries or sit
weeping, weeping in the public square
your flimsy butterfly fingers in your hair
your face destroyed by rain?

If it were you, the person you call 'I,'
the one you loved and worked for,
the most high
now become Ishmael,
might you not
grow phobias about calendars and clocks,
stare at your face in the mirror, not knowing it
and feel an identity with idiots and dogs
as all the exquisite unborns of your dreams
deserted you to snigger behind their hands?

❀ *The Sleeper*

Close the shutters of this open-faced house on a main street
so the webbed bat swings in the cornea
and the spark of the mouth sags to a summer furnace
while still, in the back garden, garrulous neighbours lean
elbows on the weak fence – their voices high
tents pitched below eye-level on the epidermal plains.

If a band goes down the avenue it goes
straight through the dozing body; the leopard skin
of the drummer who beats the ear drums
has passed through the arch of flesh, the boys of brass
shine in the solemn tunnel of trees, floodlit
with chlorophyll – flowing like fainting ones.

But now, sleeper, the neighbours and the parade are over,
the tight black bag is clipped upon your head,
you can rest a night length holding a dreadful arm up
against the brain roots filling the head with tubers.
Oh, sleeper, you can rest in a mad self-chosen bed
with a scream for a pillowslip and a bomb for bedmate.

❀ *Alice*

Mark adult Alice. Love her.
The white rabbit
nibbling leaves enters her Sunday garden,
squats on the lawn; its light-reflecting eye
like pigeon's blood on tinfoil
cocked towards her.

To Wonderland?
No. There is no such question.
Simply: the animal is out of place,
a mark for dogs and foreign in her garden.

So, she approaches.
Rabbit in the annuals
hides under leaves,
is softly quick and cunning;
dapples and dawdles under foaming flowers;
though white, is out of sight. Makes green its guardian.

The rabbit reappears.
Its fragile ears,
precarious with veins, emerge like two
pink petals with the sunlight shining through them.
Meets nemesis among nemesias.

The waiting hand descends.
Between her fingers
the ears like poppy satin crush and crumple.
No conjurer, yet full-length from the flowers
she draws her childhood wonder.

And is afraid of it.
Soft white, it struggles
more muscled than she guessed – lanugo-legged –
utterly silent. In her palm its heart
bounces a quick alary.

Oh, adult Alice,
mined with memory,
your garden's altered. Mary Quite Contrary
prods cockle-shells in every flower bed
and where you wandered coolly on the grass
a ghostly rabbit reigns supreme instead.

❀ *Paranoid*

He loved himself too much. As a child was god.
Thunder stemmed from his whims,
flowers were his path.
Throughout those early days his mother was all love,
a warm projection of him
like a second heart.

In adolescence, dark and silent, he was perfect;
still godlike and like a god
cast the world out.
Crouching in his own torso as in a chapel
the stained glass of his blood
glowed in the light.

Remained a god. Each year he grew more holy
and more wholly himself.
The self spun
thinner and thinner like a moon forming
slowly from that other self
the dead sun.

Until he was alone, revolved in ether
light years from the world,
cold and remote.
Thinking he owned the heavens too, he circled,
wanly he turned and whirled
reflecting light.

❀ *Portrait of Marina*

Far out the sea has never moved. It is
Prussian forever, rough as teaselled wool
some antique skipper worked into a frame
to bear his lost four-master.
                                   Where it hangs
now in a sunny parlour, none recalls
how all his stitches, interspersed with oaths
had made his one pale spinster daughter grow
transparent with migraines – and how his call
fretted her more than waves.
                                   Her name
Marina, for his youthful wish –
boomed at the font of that small salty church
where sailors lurched like drunkards, would, he felt
make her a water woman, rich with bells.
To her, the name Marina simply meant
he held his furious needle for her thin
fingers to thread again with more blue wool
to sew the ocean of his memory.
Now, where the picture hangs, a dimity
young inland housewife with inherited
clocks under bells and ostrich eggs on shelves
pours amber tea in small rice china cups
and reconstructs
how great-great-grandpappa at ninety-three
his fingers knotted with arthritis, his
old eyes grown agaty with cataracts
became as docile as a child again –
that fearful salty man –
and sat, wrapped round in faded paisley shawls
gently embroidering.
While Aunt Marina in grey worsted, warped
without a smack of salt, came to his call
the sole survivor of his last shipwreck.

*

Slightly offshore, it glints. Each wave is capped
with broken mirrors. Like Marina's head
the glinting of these waves.
She walked forever antlered with migraines
her pain forever putting forth new shoots
until her strange unlovely head became
a kind of candelabra – delicate –
where all her tears were perilously hung
and caught the light as waves that catch the sun.
The salt upon the panes, the grains of sand
that crunched beneath her heel
her father's voice, 'Marina!' – all these broke
her trembling edifice. The needle shook
like ice between her fingers.
In her head
too many mirrors dizzied her and broke.

                         *

But where the wave breaks, where it rises green
turns into gelatine, becomes a glass
simply for seeing stones through, runs across
the coloured shells and pebbles of the shore
and makes an aspic of them
then sucks back
in foam and undertow –
this aspect of the sea
Marina never knew.

For her the sea was Father's Fearful Sea
harsh with sea serpents
winds and drowning men.
For her it held no spiral of a shell
for her descent to dreams,
it held no bells.
And where it moved in shallows it was more
imminently a danger, more alive
than where it lay offshore full fathom five.

❀ Sailor

The kiss of death by water or desire
swam in his imagination, he
longed for the curious and cold encounter with fear.

Saw undersea as the south devoid of heat –
exotic, without scent, a clean country
demanding, calling him wherever he went.

Wanted to lose himself in its brine, instead
sailed to the easy ports like oil and lay
only on surfaces of the shallow bays.

Finally slipped from the slanting deck and spun,
hung on the air a moment like a gull
swallowed the mounting wave as it swallowed him.

And from what might have been shipwreck he was saved.
Without an element of danger came
silver in to the quiet shore –

certainly not a merman, not a ship:
man, at home, on the perilous sand
and beaded, dripping as from a sea death.

Up early on the shore line, sang, sang
as if to Christ of the waters and his song
was saline and the wave breaking his voice.

Later, like a farmer, he returned
to till his tufted field – each wave a hill,
for now his magic lay in simile.

And all his mates were sea-green novices.
Their deep unquenchable eyes, still drinking waves
wilted like foam or daisies from their thirst.

❀ Only Child

The early conflict made him pale
and when he woke from those long weeping slumbers she was there
and the air about them – hers and his –
sometimes a comfort to him, like a quilt, but more
often than not a fear.

There were times he went away – he knew not where –
over the fields or scuffing to the shore,
suffered her eagerness on his return
for news of him – where had he been, what done?
He hardly knew and didn't wish to know
or think about it vocally or share
his private world with her.

Then they would plan another walk, a long
adventure in the country, for her sake –
in search of birds. Perhaps they'd find the blue
heron today, for sure the kittiwake.

Birds were familiar to him now, he knew
them by their feathers and a shyness like his own,
soft in the silence.
By the pool she said, 'Observe,
the canvasback's a diver,' and her words
stuccoed the slaty water of the lake.

He had no wish to separate them in groups
or learn the Latin,
or, waking early to their songs remark, 'The thrush,'
or say at evening when the air is streaked
with certain swerving flying,
'Ah, the swifts.'

Birds were his element like air and not
her words for them – making them statues
setting them apart,
nor were they lots of little facts and details like a book.
When she said, 'Look!'
he let his eyeballs harden
and when two came and nested in the garden
he felt their softness, gentle, near his heart.

She gave him pictures, which he avoided, showing
them flat and coloured on a painted land.
Rather would he lie in the grass, the deep grass of the island
close to the gulls' nests, knowing
these things he loved and needed by his hand,
untouched and hardly seen but deeply understood.
Or sail among them through a wet wind feeling
their wings within his blood.

Like every mother's boy he loved and hated
smudging the future photograph she had
yet struggled within the frames of her eyes and then
froze for her, the noted naturalist –
her very affectionate and famous son.
But when most surely in her grasp, his smiles
darting and enfolding her, his words:
'Without my mother's help …' the dream occurred.

Dozens of flying things surrounded him
on a green terrace in the sun
and one by one
as if he caught caresses in his palm
he caught them all and snapped and wrung their necks
brittle as little sticks.

Then through the bald, unfeathered air
and coldly, as a man would walk
against a metal backdrop, he
bore down on her
and placed them in her wide maternal lap
and accurately said their names aloud:
woodpecker, sparrow, meadowlark, nuthatch.

❈ Snapshot

She was dime-dead,
a silver thing passed as a token from hand to hand
and where the spoken word sounded or the leaf
scratched stucco or the boy
slung the strap of his bag on a bony shoulder
and shouted down lighted avenues
she was a shadow.

Under the arc of drawing-rooms
or bending on the crooked black arm
she was quick as money
and coveted by private fingers,
fumbled for, clutched, caught and spent
in a second.

It was strange to see her alone,
lying like a wax doll on her bed
moving in a yawn of movement
staring with a flat stare
at a world of air
or caught like a bent pin
on her bedroom chair.

❀ *Neurotic*

He, in his evil cell
of root and energy
would prune the buds of love
and graft a canker
onto the floating limb
and steep the trunk
daily in brine and vinegar of thought.

But chained,
sits like a thief or monk
in innocence
and finds
the shaft of light
hit him at noontime
like a thunderbolt.

❀ Schizophrenic

Nobody knew when it would start again –
the extraordinary beast go violent in her blood;
nobody knew the virtue of her need
to shape her face to the giant in her brain.

Certainly friends were sympathetic, kind,
gave her small handkerchiefs and showed her tricks,
built her life to a sort of pick-up-sticks
simplification – as if she were a child.

Malleable she wore her lustre nails
daily like a debutante and smoked,
watching the fur her breath made as they joked,
caught like a wind in the freedom of their sails.

While always behind her face, the giant's face
struggled to break the matte mask of her skin –
and, turned about at last, be looking in –
tranquilly *in* to that imprisoned place.

Strong for the dive he dived one day at tea –
the cakes like flowers, the cups dreamy with cream –
he saw the window a lake and with a scream
nobody heard, shot by immediacy,

he forced the contours of her features out.
Her tea-time friends were statues as she passed,
pushed, but seemingly drawn towards the glass;

her tea-time friends were blind, they did not see
the violence of his struggle to get free,
and deaf, and deaf, they did not hear his shout.

The waters of his lake were sharp and cold –
splashed and broke, triangular on the floor
after the dive from his imagined shore
in a land where all the inhabitants are old.   · · ·   79

❀ Outcasts

Subjects of bawdy jokes and by the police
treated as criminals, these lovers dwell
deep in their steep albino love –
a tropic area where nothing grows.

Nobody's brothers, they revolve
on rims of the family circle, seek some place
where nothing shuns them, where no face
in greeting dons the starched immaculate mask.

Look, in their isolation they become
almost devoid of bones, their ward is one
nobody enters, but their least
window requires a curtain. They are clowns

without a private dressing room, with only
one ancient joke to crack now and forever.
They draw a crowd as if they had a band:
Always the healthy are their audiences.

The youths who hunt in packs, bitches with cash,
crafty embezzlers of the public purse,
perjurers and fashionable quacks
slumming, but saintly, saintly, judge them as

outcasts. In the laundered mind they rate
the bottom of the scale, below the Jew
with his hundred hands and pockets and below
niggers whose love is lewd.

Let doctors show a white aseptic hand
within their sickroom and let parents gaze
back against time's tight fist to find the cause –
seek in the child the answer to the man:

search out the early misfit, who at school,
sickly for love and giddy with his sex
found friendship like a door banged in his face,
his world a wasteland and himself a fool.

❀ *Foreigner*

Between strange walls
you, foreigner, walk in silence,
sheltered from eyes
by the shady hands of fear
and the suddenly dropped
blinds of embarrassment.

A room will hold you a smile
but you will not look.
From a long past of walking you have come
wearing blinkers and the balanced book.
Now pressed in a corner by words
you have no face
and cry for love
in the leaning tower of self.

❀ *Freak*

His plaster face he built as an armour,
in hands, the nerve ends nursed, and words
sieved through a fine muslin;
but never anonymous,
no, never nondescript
nor simply himself.
Always his monster.

His business: being a ten-cent joke,
a treat or terror for the kids;
beast in a marvellous cage, hanging his head
or moving his terribly funny feathery hands.
His rages, sudden and uncontrolled, bring down the house.

On big days more
popular than the tattooed lady or the giant
he feels his gift twist in his heart like a smile,
that ounce of professional pride – his glorious Christ.
And the barker a friend
and the public his personal picnic.

But away from the tent
on a holiday, not on show
everything is new
everywhere he looks, everywhere, everyone he sees
is glinting like brass
and he in their mirrors shining and bright;
locked in their light,
trapped in their pupils and pockets
and many as money.

Announced! His name,
those letters and that sound
tapped, rung out,
repeated in rain in wheels
in the wail of wind
or yelled from nowhere –
carefully spelled by an acre of empty air.

A million reflections and his heart in each
a million names called and each one his,
falling like blows on his plaster face.

He sees the cage a fine and friendly place.

❀ Man with One Small Hand

One hand is smaller than the other. It
must always be loved a little like a child;
requires attention constantly, implies
it needs his frequent glance to nurture it.

He holds it sometimes with the larger one
as adults lead a child across a street.
Finding it his and suddenly alien
rallies his interest and his sympathy.

Sometimes you come upon him unawares
just quietly staring at it where it lies
as mute and somehow perfect as a flower.

But no. It is not perfect. He admits
it has its faults: it is not strong or quick.
At night it vanishes to reappear
in dreams full-size, lost or surrealist.

Yet has its place like memory or a dog –
is never completely out of mind – a rod
to measure all uncertainties against.

Perhaps he loves it too much, sets too much stock
simply in its existence. Ah, but look!
It has its magic. See how it will fit
so sweetly, sweetly in the infant's glove.

❀ *Isolationist*

When the many move, the man
in the cubicle of content
cowers, suddenly discovered, suddenly rent
by the reality of crowds.
He has trained the climbing vine,
written 'roses' on his ledger,
lived like a saint and finds himself a leper.

Immaculate of belief and violent on Mondays,
thinking no evil and thanking no second party
he has leaned in the evenings on the low-lipped window
and learned of his saintliness from outlines of lovers.

Now lovers leap the sash and the many winnow
his penny bank of wisdom and set it swirling
down the unclogged drain in the hidden scullery.
People take solid shape and are vividly human,
smash walls, uproot chairs and juggle cutlery
while he sits with gloved hands in a buttoned confusion.

❀ *The Sick*

All these, the horizontal and inactive,
held in the fronds of fever
or crooks of pain,
with their many pupilled and respective
eyes floating like water flowers on a stagnant river
or tight and walled as stone,
inhabit a country that is all their own.

Lie on the personal white plains of beds
but not as sleepers do,
giving themselves,
nor yet as lovers, windmills in their heads;
but emptied out as hoof-prints where the cattle go,
they live, pathetic halves,
pallidly hoping to complete themselves.

Some in the levitation of half sleep
with heads like dandelions
seeded and soft
have lost their bodies as they lost their hopes
and float like freaks in air – pneumatic scions –
inflated by a cough
to altitudes where there is nothing left.

Others as white as nurses, clean as soap,
drift in a scent of pink
with roses nudging them
into a patent and elastic sleep
where they can soar with suns before they sink
below the nurses' hems
single and cool and fresh as roses' stems.

While all the others in the coal-hole dark,
lighting their own despair
and unattended
except by bills and fears about their work,
are pale as oysters when exposed to air
and illness ended,
the thing that's broken in them is not mended.

For loneliness and fear signal like scouts
in jumping semaphore
from head to heart,
or joined, light flares and never put them out
and from the dying ones, set fire to more;
so, single as a dart
the body is; as single as a dart

and yet is multiple, rubs shoulders with
twins at each corner
shakes its own hands
while meeting foreigners and living myths
and rarely knows itself to be the owner
of common dividends
through having interest in a hundred lands.

❀ *Probationer*

Floats out of anaesthetic
helium hipped
a bird a bride your breath could bruise,
is blurred.

Re-forms in bright enamel, tiny, chips
into recurring selves
a hundred of her
giving you smiles and small white pills of water.

Grows in delirium as striped and strange
as any tiger crouching in the flowers.
Her metal finger tip
taps out your pulse.

Intrinsic to your pain
lives in its acre
and only there because your wound has made her,
beyond its radius she has never been.

Is sly and clever suddenly, creates
you wholly out of sheets and air – full-grown.
Most wonderfully makes a halo of your hair.
Gives you a name – your own.

Oh, in the easy mornings comes with smiles,
tipping the window so it spills the sun
carries the basin plastic with slipping water
and calls it fun.

For she is only a girl. And crisis over
she is herself again – clumsy and gauche,
her jokes too hearty
and her touch too rough.

And by a slow dissolve
becomes at last,
someone you've always known –
yourself perhaps.

Yet alters when you leave. From her stiff starch
she overflows in laughs, is proud and shy
and as if you are a present she has made,
she gives you away.

❀ *Element*

Feeling my face has the terrible shine of fish
caught and swung on a line under the sun
I am frightened, held in the light that people make
and sink in darkness freed and whole again
as fish returned by dream into the stream.

Oh, running water is not rough: ruffled to eye,
to flesh it's flat and smooth; to fish
silken as children's hands in milk.

I am not wishful in this dream of immersion.
Mouth becomes full with darkness
and the shine, mottled and pastel, sounds its own note, not
the fake high treble thrown on resounding faces.

There are flowers – and this is pretty for the summer –
light on the bed of darkness; there are stones
that glisten and grow slime;
winters that question nothing, are a new
night for the passing movement of fine fins;
and quietly, by the reeds or the water fronds
something can cry without discovery.

Ah, in daylight the shine is single
as dime flipped or gull on fire or fish
silently hurt – its mouth alive with metal.

❀ *Sleeper*

The ritual of bedtime takes its shape
meadowed with sheets and hilled with pillows plumped
for head's indenture –
oh, the prairie air's plangent with scent of soap.

Now, silken, smooth, the body stretches out
easy with sleep;
beneath the lazy hand
print that eye has sprinted on grows fur
to stroke a milky eye.

Light goes with an explosion.
In the head
colours remain like ribbons –
drift and blow;
move and are static, fill a floating frame,
flow over and re-form in fern and sand.

The gentle dreamer drowns without a sound
softly in eiderdown.
Almost, he dies.
As divers who are dead, his body floats
pneumatic on black tides.

Complete in sleep, discards his arms and legs
with only whimpers;
from his flesh retreats
like water through a mesh, leaving it beached
alone upon a bed.

And takes the whole night in his lungs and head.
A hydrocephalic idiot, quick at sums
wandering strangely lost and loose among
symbols as blunted and as bright as flowers.

✿ *Nightmare*

In the white bed
this too dark creature nests,
litters her yelping young
upon my breasts.

Dreams are her thicket.
In them, wearing masks
of my familiar faces,
she dissembles.

Trembles in every image
calls my falcon
which falls, a feathered stone
to her white wrist bone.

Twists me like wire,
stretches me tight and thin,
a black skeleton stark
among flowering apples.

Or, an appalling valentine
of lace and hearts
hot and frilled,
abandoned in the sun

do I become
at the dark bitter wish
of this night-walking
anxious alchemist.

Sometimes she smiles at me
as if I were
her own face
smiling in a mirror

and she rehearsing
sweet looks in my eyes
of barley sugar
and of butterflies.

Yet should I sleep forever
she would eat
my beating heart
as if it were a plum

did she not know
with terrible wisdom
by doing so
she would devour her own.

❋ *Subjective Eye*

When the sleeping eye awakes –
tiger turned turtle
withdrawn within its shell –
before it sheds the personal attack
dreams made upon it, smudging with their symbols
its outward focus,
while carrying in it still
barbs and barbiturates
as yet unpearled,
then all the fat air and the greenest morning
with a perfect parliament of leaves
is not.
And eye, poor potentate,
its kingdom shrunk
from rolling round of earth to round of pupil
is smoked as though a cataract had formed
not over it, but over the green world.

❀ The Dreamer

The dreamer walks like a conjurer onto the stage,
his promises a formula,
sleight of hand
silvers the air and the band
sounds like a pier band –
different and sharp and near.

Nothing is hard but the present chair –
the tricks
click and snap and float like balloons and fill
nebulous eyes with colour
while the band
plays in the pit of the inner and outer ear.

Calls an accomplice, conjurer does, and you
are party to dreams;
he pulls them out of your mouth
like fancy handkerchiefs
or a string of beads.
From a zippered pocket of flesh
a rabbit grins.

Strip him, audience,
turn out his pockets, tear
his crazy clothes from his back,
while the band continues
fainter now in a tent of paper streamers.
Expose his tricks
and the muscles of his hands
and see him, pink and blue as litmus paper,
clutching at cardboard or a piece of string.

Generation

(i)

❀ *Landlady*

Through sepia air the boarders come and go
impersonal as trains. Pass silently
the craving silence swallowing her speech;
click doors like shutters on her camera eye.

Because of her their lives become exact:
their entrances and exits are designed;
phone calls are cryptic. Oh, her ticklish ears
advance and fall back stunned.

Nothing is unprepared. They hold the walls
about them when they weep or laugh. Each face
is dialled to zero publicly. She peers
stippled with curious flesh;

pads on the patient landing like a pulse,
unlocks their keyholes with the wire of sight,
searches their rooms for clues when they are out,
pricks when they come home late.

Wonders when they are quiet, jumps when they move,
dreams that they dope or drink, trembles to know
the traffic of their brains, jaywalks their street
in clumsy shoes.

Yet knows them better than their closest friends:
their cupboards and the secrets of their drawers,
their books, their private mail, their photographs
are theirs and hers.

Knows when they wash, how frequently their clothes
go to the cleaners, what they like to eat,
their curvature of health, but even so
is not content,

and, like a lover, must know all, all, all.
Prays she may catch them unprepared at last
and palm the dreadful riddle of their skulls –
hoping the worst.

❀ Bed-Sitting Room

The sun has beaten its palms flat against glass.
Getting no answer, strides like a long-legged ghost
over the windowsill and camps on the rug;
releases canaries, which perch on the chair and table,
hang from a bow on the wallpaper
and sing like a needle.

The woman is cramped in the cupboard of ancient moths,
fondles the smudge of air with a face-cloth face,
breathes down the neck of her blouse
telling her threat of beads
with pin-prick fingers.

In the drawer her friends are launching their own Armadas
of paper boats with home-truth ammunition;
the photos duel in their frames,
the smiling boy
hurls his smile like a javelin at the mirror.
The friend who will sit in the South of France forever
has shot her eyes at the class of nineteen thirty.

In the medicine closet behind the screen, the doctor
squats on his own prescription, legs round a bottle,
numb with his game and stiff as a flagpole sitter;

the authors scream to be set free from their prison.

❀ *Offices*

Oh, believe me, I have known offices –
young and old in them, both –
morning and evening;
felt the air
stamp faces into a mould;
office workers at desks
saying *go* to a typewriter
and *stop* to a cabinet;
taking scrupulous care over calendars
so days
are etched in the outward-leaning eyes
while bosses, behind glass like jewels,
are flashing their light and coming suddenly near.

In offices drawers contain
coloured paper for copies,
staples, string,
hand lotion and various personal things
like love letters.

In washrooms girls are pretty with their mouths,
drawing them fancy; light the sugar-white tube of smoke
and never once question the future, look ahead
beyond payday or ask the *if* that makes them angular.

In elevators, coming and going, they are glib-
tongued and perky as birds with the elevator men.
Some, beautiful and coloured always, like singing,
never become the permanent collection
and some – if you speak to them of a different world,
a future more like life – become sharp,
give you their whittled face
and turn away like offended starlings from a wind.

❀ *Prediction without Crystal*

Oh, you girls, with your sad eyes and your visions
of fortune-tellers floating in the pond of the crystal
or breathing on your palms in the electric
moment of seeing marriage written surely,

dreaming the silent room where the gypsied woman
flicks dirty cards by the cluttered paper roses,
juggles with love and conjures up initials –

girls in your leisure hours, awkward at parties,
gaming with sugar dice and casting caution
into the cockle-shell of the secret cauldron,

there is no private world, I tell you truly,
no single room for you except the lonely
room of yourselves. I can predict your futures:

bandstand your bacchanals, the blackened alleys
bright for you, cock-crow your reveille
and darkness your desired and nimble dodger;

you'll walk like a crow along the winter furrow
wild in a world of day and mean with terror
while hips and cheekbones squeak and totter narrow

then run from newsreel, strike and strychnine street
into the room of *you* and die in mirrors
for click and close the camera covers lovers.

❀ The Stenographers

After the brief bivouac of Sunday,
their eyes, in the forced march of Monday to Saturday,
hoist the white flag, flutter in the snowstorm of paper,
haul it down and crack in the midsun of temper.

In the pause between the first draft and the carbon
they glimpse the smooth hours when they were children –
the ride in the ice-cart, the ice-man's name,
the end of the route and the long walk home;

remember the sea where floats at high tide
were sea marrows growing on the scatter-green vine
or spools of grey toffee, or wasps' nests on water;
remember the sand and the leaves of the country.

Bell rings and they go and the voice draws their pencil
like a sled across snow; when its runners are frozen
rope snaps and the voice then is pulling no burden
but runs like a dog on the winter of paper.

Their climates are winter and summer – no wind
for the kites of their hearts – no wind for a flight;
a breeze at the most, to tumble them over
and leave them like rubbish – the boy-friends of blood.

In the inch of the noon as they move they are stagnant.
The terrible calm of the noon is their anguish;
the lip of the counter, the shapes of the straws
like icicles breaking their tongues are invaders.

Their beds are their oceans – salt water of weeping
the waves that they know – the tide before sleep;
and fighting to drown they assemble their sheep
in columns and watch them leap desks for their fences
and stare at them with their own mirror-worn faces.

In the felt of the morning the calico-minded,
sufficiently starched, insert papers, hit keys,
efficient and sure as their adding machines;
yet they weep in the vault, they are taut as net curtains
stretched upon frames. In their eyes I have seen
the pin men of madness in marathon trim
race round the track of the stadium pupil.

❀ Typists

They, without message, having read
the running words on their machines,
know every letter as a stamp
cutting the stencils of their ears.
Deep in their hands, like pianists,
all longing gropes and moves, is trapped
behind the tensile gloves of skin.

Or, blind, sit with their faces locked
away from work. Their varied eyes
stiff as everlasting flowers.
While fingers on a different plane
perform the automatic act
as questions grope along the dark
and twisting corridors of brain.

Crowded together typists touch
softly as ducks and seem to sense
each others' anguish with the swift
sympathy of the deaf and dumb.

❀ *Shipbuilding Office*

The strange jargon of ships and their building
floats very lightly, like flotsam
in heads stormily holding the perilous oceans of love.
They are like children at desks,
their farthest eyes tracing
the angle of a first flight,
their nearest ones reading
with uncanny accuracy and no perception
contracts for hawser wire
boilers and cable.

This girl in gingham,
shy as a traitor
her face hardly emerged
from the dive of childhood,
rides the clock with spurs through ship and dock;
unrelated as fable
to nineteen forty,
her job, her jargon
or the permanent carbon
fixing eight sets of everything angrily upon paper.

❀ *The Petition*

Unplanned as love the petition was written,
signed, and the room altered.

Sun went unacknowledged,
wind wanted for attention;
carpenters tapping and boring
in proximate walls
emptied in silence
when the clumsy blood
climbed the precipice of the body
and stamped in the lookout.

Friends were unfrocked;
girls who had held
each other's hands like lovers,
always in pairs,
and prattled secrets, secrets
in the coils of ears,
drew apart like knives,
were whetted on belief.

Enemies released
the tight cord of dislike,
knitted the space between desks
in the bright office.
Grew firm without speech as they felt
the wall of decision
and fear like a runner devour
the race-tracks of blood in their flesh.

Waiting, the afternoon
limped untidily; time
tottered and fainted and fell
in the uneven room
through the cross-checked hours
as no response or reply
dotted the screaming i's
of their clamouring signatures.

❀ *Presentation*

Now most miraculously the most junior clerk
becomes a hero.
Oh, beautiful child
projected suddenly to executive grandeur,
gone up like an angel in the air of good wishes,
the gift and the speeches.

Dry as chalk from your files you come, unfolding.
In the hothouse they have made of their hearts
you flower
and by the double magic, force their flower –
the gift repaid in the symbol of desire.
You have become quite simply glorious.
They by comparison cannot be less.

Oh, lighted by this dream, the office glows
brightly among the double row of desks.
This day shines in their breasts like emeralds,
their faces wake from sleeping as you smile.
They have achieved new grace because you leave.
Each, at this moment, has a home, has love.

❀ *Summer Resort*

They lie on beaches and are proud to tan –
climb banks in search of flowers for their hair,
change colours like chameleons and seem
indolent and somehow flat and sad.

Search out the trees for love, the beach umbrellas,
the bar, the dining-room; flash as they walk,
are pretty-mouthed and careful as they talk;
send picture post-cards to their offices
brittle with ink and soft with daily phrases.

Find Sunday empty without churches – loll
not yet unwound in deck chair and by pool,
cannot do nothing neatly, while in lap,
periscope ready, scan the scene for love.

Under the near leaves or the sailing water
eyes hoist flags and handkerchiefs between the breasts, alive,
flutter like pallid bats at the least eddy.

Dread the return that magnifies the want –
wind in high places soaring round the heart
and carried like a star-fish in a pail
through dunes and fields and lonely mountain paths.

But memory, which is thinner than the senses,
is only a wave in grass that the kiss erases,
and love once found, their metabolism changes:
the kiss is worn like a badge upon the mouth –
pinned there in darkness, emphasized in daylight.

Now all the scene is flying. Before the face
people and trees are swift; the enormous pool
brims like a crying eye. The immediate flesh
is real and night no curtain.

There, together, the swift exchange of badges
accelerates to a personal prize-giving
while pulse and leaf rustle and grow climactic.

❀ *The Inarticulate*

Dumb are their tongues and doubtful their belief.
And grown too slow to speak,
grow double dumb,
misers of words and miserable when wrapped
tight in a sentence.
(O move the comma half an inch for head
to slip and wriggle through –
the final latch
clicks with the word of sense.)

I see them daily, inarticulate,
on streetcar and on street;
work at their desks
and worm my hearing underneath their skulls,
die from the silence rooted in their tongues,
slide like a cup upon their screaming eyes
and feel the sirens blowing in their necks
vibrate too high for sound.

They wither, tuned for sound, who cannot speak,
hammer all day at keys that do not print,
and file their voices in the teeming vault.
Learning the language of the deaf and dumb
their prayers are lit, but studying fingers creak.
Like foreign papers, no one reads their hands.

❁ *Panorama*

In quick panorama with parasol, parrot and panda;
saying perhaps or because,
eating pink end of match
and with pastel tissue for lavatory use
and deparlourized parlour
and cheddar the lamplight of love
they dissolve upon chairs,
write ruin in pearls
on the flesh of inherited faith
and famish in pairs.

They attend us in dreams and in droves
like a filigree shade,
fall down between us and our time
prick the drum with their tune
and fence the inviolate field
with the quick of their eyes.

❀ Bank Strike

Quebec, 1942

When the time came,
after the historied waiting,
they were ready with their strikers' jackets
and their painted signs 'En Grève,'
facing the known streets
and the rough serge knees and elbows
of police.

Time was bald on their skins,
their desks and counters and cages
cried in their eyes like a strategical retreat
and the unrelieved picket line
had a stained, for-all-time permanence
on the distorted street.

In the foreground church
the flames of the sacred candles
burned, in their suddenly foreign homes
their meals were stiff as religious paintings
and the bullet of 'fired'
was wedged in their skulls.

Yet from the cellar of certainty they came
up the long escalator to defeat,
their hearts hurting their ribs, their hands heavy;
blew hot and cold
and scratched the solid curb
like weather worrying an iron city.

❀ *Squatters*

So orderly was their conduct it was as if
chessmen had suddenly moved of their own accord
under beneficent darkness across the stiff
squares of the board.

Tired of waiting for the hovering hands'
strategic gestures, for the minds' approved
consideration, they made their demands
and received the inadequate answers before they moved.

Entered the empty house without right of entry,
a phosphorescence issuing from their action,
feeling at last they entered their own country
from a new direction.

Were citizens and individuals once
they became a community; they understood
the clear simplicity of omnipotence
in planning from common need for a common good.

But they had committed the most outrageous act:
they were neither violent nor tough,
every action had been circumspect.
Obviously they could not be hated enough.

❊ The Permanent Tourists

Somnolent through landscapes and by trees
nondescript, almost anonymous,
they alter as they enter foreign cities –
the terrible tourists with their empty eyes
longing to be filled with monuments.

Verge upon statues in the public squares
remembering the promise of memorials
yet never enter the entire event
as dogs, abroad in any kind of weather,
move perfectly within their rainy climate.

Lock themselves into snapshots on the steps
of monolithic bronze as if suspecting
the subtle mourning of the photograph
might, later, conjure in the memory
all they are now incapable of feeling.

And track all heroes down: the boy who gave
his life to save a town: the stolid queen;
forgotten politicians minus names;
the plunging war dead, permanently brave,
forever and ever going down to death.

Look, you can see them nude in any café
reading their histories from the bill of fare,
creating futures from a foreign teacup.
Philosophies like ferns bloom from the fable
that travel is broadening at the café table.

Yet, somehow beautiful, they stamp the plaza.
Classic in their anxiety they call
all the memorials of naked stone
into their passive eyes, as placid rivers
are always calling to the ruined columns.

❀ *Average*

These fishes take their own trip, scrape
sun from wave's underside with fin,
while eyes – rock-crystal – see two sets of things:
the right and left with equal clarity,
so held, retain their changeless courses, swim
in chilled and judgeless equilibrium.

Move wholly without implication, skate
solely on their single blade through all
that makes them fish – courtyard and corridor
of brine and coral and the fretwork shade
of salty forests blossoming with shells.

Yet only are concerned with what they eat,
nosing the silent waterways and weeds;
defend by camouflage when danger is death,
glide off in steel for any other threat
to spread the news abroad through wave and spout
that raiders are about.

❀ Quarrel

Now at the counter the cups have clanked on the marble –
tea like a solid bar has drilled the cup
as women poured it fiercely from the pot,
their mouths burnt and their eyes like flies on paper.

Bound to each other by anger they sit as sisters
sometimes sit who have nothing to say yet cling
to their closeness as though to a speaking thing
and so grow old together and never notice.

So these have aged in the minutes binding them:
muscles are wood and ligaments are stiff
until, their anger gradually wearing off,
they are suddenly delicate as girls again.

❋ *Election Day*

1.

I shut the careful door of my room and leave
letters, photographs and the growing poem –
the locked zone of my tight and personal thought
slough off – recede from down the green of the street.
Naked almost among the trees and wet –
a strike for lightning.

And everything rushes at me, either fierce or friendly
in a sudden world of bulls.
Faces on posters in the leaves call out
the violent *yes* or *no* to my belief,
are quick or slow or halted to my pulse.

Oh, on this beautiful day, the weather wooing
the senses and the feel of walking
smooth in my summer legs
I lope through the tall and trembling grass and call
the streaming banner of my public colour.

2.

Here in this place, the box and private privet
denote the gentleman and shut him in –
for feudally he lives and the feud on.
Colonel Evensby with his narrow feet
will cast his blue-blood ballot for the Tory

and in the polling station I shall meet
the smiling, rather gentle overlords
propped by their dames and almost twins in tweeds,
and mark my X against them and observe
my ballot slip, a bounder, in the box.

And take my route again through the lazy streets
alive with all-out blossoming, through trees
that stint no colour for their early summer
and past an empty lot where an old dog
appoints himself as guardian of the green.

   3.

Radio owns my room as the day ends.
The slow returns begin, the voice calls
the yeses and the noes that ring or toll;
the districts all proclaim themselves in turn
and public is my room, not personal.

Midnight. I wander on the quiet street,
its green swamped by the dark; a pale glow
sifts from the distant lamps. Behind the leaves
the faces on the posters wait and blow,
tattered a little and less urgent now.

I pass the empty lot. The old dog
has trotted off to bed. The neighbourhood
is neatly hedged with privet still, the lights
are blinking out in the enormous homes.
Gentlemen, for the moment, you may sleep.

❀ *Prophecy*

Now the quick city which throws up ladders like fountains
climbs them constantly
ascending in squares
has succeeded in shooting the sun
from so close a range
that electric light is constant
and nothing like day can polish a bay
or pipe an eye with silver.

Now faces are marionettes
made at the end of a dinner
from serviettes
called to dance between candles
or play with food.
There are offices for their daytime pleasure
and carts to pull
and prams are piled in the well of the tenement stairs
crawling with ancient children
and quick with cries.

Now the long streets have become a terror
are part of a maze
and murderers police them at their leisure
with sherbet roses in their soft lapels.
The dead are lining the streets and no one cares.
The dead are walking the streets and no one stares.

❈ No Flowers

You who have floated on bored water among the islands,
who have stopped for the length of a highball, the length of a tea,
at ports you cannot remember or only remember
by the shape of the sandwiches and cocktail napkins;
you who have always cruised on the luxury liner,
do you find comfort in the tiled bathrooms on this sea?

You have faithfully tipped the stewards but will they serve you
with equal faithfulness when the ship is sinking?
The steamer rug and the deck-chair in the sun
are little to cling to when the deck creaks down.
No hand-made shoes can reincarnate Peter
and Elizabeth Arden cannot withstand salt water.
Your face under the wave will be
pitiful as the little lackey's
and the initialled suitcase you pack and save
will only precipitate the gall-green grave.

There will be no laying out on the shell-ribbed bed;
no undertaker with fat white breath
to comb the feather hair or stick the pin
into the gilt-edged stock beneath the chin;
and no old woman will come with guttering hands
to seal your eyes with pennies and no old man
will need to press the tired ball of his foot
sharp on the spade to dig the hallowed spot.

Octopus arms will hold you and sea snails
will stud the lobes of your ears;
the wide blade of the water will pare your hips
down to a size sixteen – the coveted size;
and starfish, swept by wakes of other ships,
will cast their angular shapes across your eyes.

❀ *Knitters*

These women knitting knit a kind of mist –
climate of labyrinth –
into the air.
Sitting like sleepers,
propped against the chintz,
pin-headed somehow – figures by Moore –
arachnes in their webs, they barely stir –

except their eyes and hands, which wired to some
urgent personal circuit,
move as if
a switch controlled them.
Hear the click and hum
as their machines translating hieroglyphs,
compulsive and monotonous, consume –
lozenge and hank – the candy-coloured stuff.

See two observe the ceremony of skeins:
one, forearms raised,
the loops around her palms,
cat's-cradle rocks, is metronome, becalmed;
while her companion
spun from her as from
a wooden spindle, winds a woollen world.

A man rings like an axe, is alien,
imperilled by them,
finds them cold and far.
They count their stitches on a female star
and speak another language,
are not kin.
Or is he Theseus remembering
that maze, those daedal ways; the Minotaur?

They knit him out, the wool grows thick and fills
the room they sit in like a fur
as vegetable more than animal,
surrealist and slightly sinister,
driven by motors strong beyond their wills,
these milky plants devour
more hanks of wool, more cubic feet of air.

✸ The Sentimental Surgeon

Watch him perform – the sentimental surgeon –
anaesthetize with scent
the dying patient,
hide raw hand in the pastel glove.
Diagnosis proclaims the operation urgent,
yet flowers float sadly in his salon face
where tense and straining at their tendon traces
should crouch the whippets of love.

Sickle of students swings and is suspended,
sees his evasion
to make the incision,
sees fruit knife whetted on the strop of sleeve;
knowing that already the lesson is ended,
the promise – a pastiche of sound and scent
mixed with a tray of useless instruments –
the sickle breaks and leaves.

Ready at last, the square of flesh exposed,
he holds the smiling knife,
and lean with grief,
draws an artistic line upon the patient;
reflexes curl the clusters of his toes,
he turns away and suffers – plucked, his eyes,
the petals saying 'no-yes-no,' he cries
in the enamel basin.

Nurse who is pledged to serve and make no sound
is standing by with sponge
while her rebellious lungs
are bright with anger and her molten lips
welded. He whispers to the wound;
softly, as butter melts, he operates –
taps, pats and probes; when faced with fact escapes
through flabby nerves and pitying fingertips.

Sutures, relieved, with lazy-daisy stitch,
is pleased and smiles
as when a child
he made a needle case for his frail mother;
checks the desire to finish with a kiss
and weeping sees the supine body rolled
backward to poison and infect a world
as it unwraps from ether.

*

The ailing patient wears away the bed.
Not being healed
or adequately killed
death pangs and life are dangerously convergent.
Asleep he puts the bell beneath his head,
awake he watches with some extra eye
the mountains of his health's geography
and waits the daily visit of his surgeon.

(ii)

❊ *Generation*

Schooled in the rubber bath,
promoted to scooter
early, to evade and dart;
learning our numbers
adequately, with a riveting tongue;
freed from the muddle of sex
by the never-mention method
and treading
the treacherous tightrope
of unbelieved religion,
we reached the dreadful
opacity of adolescence.

We were an ignored
and undeclared ultimatum
of solid children;
moving behind our flesh
like tumblers on the lawn
of an unknown future,
taking no definite shape –
shifting and merging
with an agenda
of unanswerable questions
growing like roots.

Tragically, Spain was our spade;
the flares went up in the garden.
We dug at night;
the relics within the house
sagged.
Walking down country lanes
we committed arson –
firing our parent-pasts;

on the wooded lands
our childhood games grew real:
the police and robbers
held unsmiling faces
against each other.

We strapped our hands in slings
fearing the dreaded
gesture of compromise:
became a war,
knew love roll from a bolt
long as the soil
and, loving, saw
eyes like our own
studding the map like cities.

Now we touch continents
with our little fingers,
swim distant seas
and walk on foreign streets
wearing crash helmets
of permanent beliefs.

❀ *Cullen*

Cullen renounced his cradle at fifteen,
set the thing rocking with his vanishing foot
hoping the artifice would lessen the shock.
His feet were tender as puffballs on the stones.

He explored the schools first and didn't understand
the factory-made goods they stuffed in his mind
or why the gramophone voice always ran down
before it reached the chorus of its song.
Corridors led 'from' but never 'to,'
stairs were merely an optical illusion,
in the damp basement where they hung their coats
he cried with anger and was called a coward.
He didn't understand why they were taught
life was good by faces that said it was not.
He discovered early 'the writing on the wall'
was dirty words scrawled in the shadowy hall.

Cullen wrote a note on his plate with the yolk of his egg
saying he hardly expected to come back,
and then, closing his textbooks quietly,
took his personal legs into the city.
Toured stores and saw the rats beneath the counters
(he visited the smartest shopping centres)
saw the worm's bald head rise in clerks' eyes
and metal lips spew out fantasies.
Heard the time clock's tune and the wage's pardon,
saw dust in the storeroom swimming towards the light
in the enormous empty store at night;
young heads fingering figures and floating freights
from hell to hell with no margin for mistakes.

Cullen bent his eye and paid a price
to sit on the mountain of seats like edelweiss –

watched the play pivot, discovered his escape
and with the final curtain went backstage;
found age and sorrow were an application,
beauty a mirage, fragrance fictionary,
the ball dress crumpled, sticky with grease and sweat.
He forgot to close the stage door as he went.

He ploughed the city, caught on a neon sign,
heard the noise of machines talking to pulp,
found the press treacherous as a mountain climb:
all upper case required an alpenstock.
Tried out the seasons then, found April cruel –
there had been no Eliot in his books at school –
discovered that stitch of knowledge on his own
remembering all the springs he had never known.
Summer grew foliage to hide the scar,
bore leaves that looked as light as tissue paper
leaves that weighed as heavy as a plate.
Fall played a flute and stuck it in his ear,
Christmas short-circuited and fired a tree
with lights and baubles; hid behind Christ; unseen
counted its presents on an adding-machine.

Cullen renounced the city, nor did he bother
to leave the door ajar for his return;
found his feet willing and strangely slipping like adders
away from the dreadful town.
Decided country, which he had never seen
was carillon greenness lying behind the eyes
and ringing the soft warm flesh behind the knees;
decided that country people were big and free.
Found himself lodgings with fishermen on a cliff,
slung his hammock from these beliefs and slept.

Morning caught his throat when he watched the men
return at dawn like silver-armoured Vikings
to women malleable as rising bread.
At last, the environment was to his liking.
Sea was his mirror and he saw himself
twisted as rope and fretted with the ripples;
concluded quietness would comb him out:
for once, the future managed to be simple.

He floated a day in stillness, felt the grass
grow in his arable body, felt the gulls
trace the tributaries of his heart and pass
over his river beds from feet to skull.
He settled with evening like a softening land
withdrew his chair from the sun the oil lamp made,
content to rest within his personal shade.
The women, gathering, tatted with their tongues
shrouds for their absent neighbours and the men
fired with lemon extract and bootlegged rum
suddenly grew immense.
No room could hold them – he was overrun,
trampled by giants, his grass was beaten down.
Nor could his hammock bear him, for it hung
limp from a single nail, salty as kelp.

Cullen evacuated overnight,
he knew no other region to explore;
discovered it was nineteen thirty-nine
and volunteered at once and went to war
wondering what on earth he was fighting for.
He knew there was a reason but couldn't find it
and marched to battle half an inch behind it.

❁ *Forgive Us*

Forgive us, who have not
been whole or rich as fruit;
who, through the eyes' lock enter
a point beyond the centre
to find our balance shot;

who have, if we confessed,
observed, but never guessed
what lies behind the fact:
the quiet, incipient act
that alters all the rest.

Those of us who took
the style to be the book,
the incident as all
and unequivocal,
must take another look.

Our blueprint was at fault.
The edifice we built
disintegrates and falls:
haunting its ruined halls
the spectre of our guilt.

That kindergarten ghost
is suddenly our host
and, once we're wined and dined,
wants to be paid in kind
and fast becomes our guest.

❈ *The Event*

The keys all turned to that event
as if it were a magnetic lock.
A rush of streams flowed into it
thundering from the great divide
while numberless and hidden heads
like flowers leaned out to feel its light.

The lion, somnolent with food,
the bear in his continuing winter,
rose to its bell as if their blood
conveyed its red and vital current.
That instant the indifferent street
became their sudden food.

Lilies and archangels began
the gradual gentling of the lion.
The burred bear fell asleep again –
a snowfall lulled him to a lamb.
Like velvet toys they lie there prone
and dream the cactus plant of pain.

But children will be born whose blood
remembers that event.
The lion and bear will waken up
ravenous after sleep
and lilies then will be their bread,
archangels their white meat.

❀ *Puppets*

See them joined by strings to history:
their strange progenitors all born full-grown,
ancestors buried with the ancient Greeks –
slim terra-cotta dolls with articulate limbs
lying like corpses.
                Puppets in Rome
subject to papal laws, discreet in tights.

And see the types perpetuate themselves
freed from the picket prejudice of race:
the seaside Punch with his inherited nose
carried from Pulcinella round the globe
ends up in Bexhill, enters English eyes.

While here in a Sunday drawing room beside
the bland Pacific and its rain, come two
emerging full-grown from their dark cocoons –
two whose blasé antecedents once
performed for Pepys's mistress, or, in silk,
were bawdy for bored royalty at court;
escaped and raided country fairs and spread
the world with areas of Lilliput.

Before our eyes the twelve-inch clown grows large
and dances on his rubber feet and kicks
pneumatic legs, thumbs his enormous nose;
lies down for push-ups – and, exhibitionist –
suddenly turns and waves.
More clown than clowns he is all laughter, is
buoyed by it and brilliant in its light.
Unlike his living prototype has no
dichotomy to split him: this is all.
He calls your laughter out without reserve –
is only and always feet and a vulgar streak
and his music, brass.

The negro does a tap-dance and his toes
click on the parquet.
Music moves in him and explodes in his toes
and somehow he is twofold, though he grins.
His hands are stripped of humour,
they are long
and lonely attached to him.
He is himself and his own symbol,
sings
terribly without a voice, is so
gentle it seems that his six delicate strings
are ropes upon him.
But still he grins, he grins.

Oh, coming isolated from their plays but not
isolated from their history,
shaped and moulded by heredity,
negro and clown in microcosm, these
small violent people shake the quiet room
and bring all history tumbling about
a giant audience that almost weeps.

❀ Waking

I lie in the long parenthesis of arms
dreaming of love
and the crying cities of Europe

wake to the bird a whistler in my room
and sun a secret.

Light on the bed of air
and buoyed by morning
the easy bugle of breath
projects an echo

while over the difficult room
the brimming window
opens the bandaged eyes
to the shape of Asia.

Invalid, I –
and crippled by sleep's illness,
drowned in the milk of sheets
and silk of dreams,
I rise and write the rising curve of day
with mercury of the smashed thermometer
and trouble the silent mirror, who have been
pale in suspension on the oval bed.

❀ *Paradox*

Let us by paradox
choose a Catholic close
for innocence.
Wince at the smell
of beaded flowers
like rosaries on the bush.
Let us stand together then
till the cool evening
settles this silent place
and having seen the hatted priest
walk with book from presbytery to border
and the pale nuns, handless as seals,
move in the still shadow,
let us stand here close,
for death is common as grass beyond an ocean,
and, with all Europe pricking in our eyes,
suddenly remember Guernica
and be gone.

❀ *Migration*

Now in this season there are no words left:
they have all walked off on their bird legs
they have all walked off on their sticks and stilts
on their matches of makeshift.

And where they were, the snow lies
and the silent argueless plains stretch
starkly unmapped with their migration.

And where they were are bird feet
marked in the snow like ghostly fossils
while above and perpendicular
as if their going scarred the air
their thin legs unattached to bodies
are walking swiftly
are white scratches
catching the shadows
like slight scratches
etching the pupil.

And all retreating
and all jerking
spastic, truncated,
and all retreating.

❀ *Draughtsman*

He wears his eyes a tattered blue on charts,
watches from square to careful square, the slow
and formless fading of his art.
'For thirty years or more,' he says and stares
far-sightedly at what is there before his nose.

'Space held about by lines,' he says, 'by thin
accurate lines my hand draws on the cloth,
held in and chequered by me all these years –
made like a building almost – lines like steel,
girders against the weight and wind, but cramped.
Space held too tight and close,' he says and squints
near-sightedly at what is dim and far.

Fear sits upon his draughting board. His hands
shake as he rules those old straight lines; his prints
don't come so clean now from the quick machine.
Approached, he parries with the laugh he hates
and feels the bottle's beautiful liquid shape
cool in the memory of his youthful palms.

While all the time his fading vision shifts
and far is hot and near, and near so far.

❀ *Some There Are Fearless*

In streets where pleasure grins
and the bowing waiter
turns double somersaults to the table for two
and the music of the violin is a splinter
pricking the poultice of flesh; where glinting glass
shakes with falsetto laughter,
Fear, the habitué, ignores the menu
and plays with his finger bowl at his permanent table.

Tune in the ear: in tub, in tube, in cloister
he is the villain; underneath the bed,
bare-shanked and shaking; drunken in pubs; or teaching
geography to half a world of children.

In times like these, in streets like these, in alleys,
he is the master and they run for shelter
like ants to ant hills when he lifts his rattle.
While dreaming wishful dreams that will be real,
some there are, fearless, touching a distant thing –
the ferreting sun, the enveloping shade, the attainable spring,
and the wonderful soil, nameless, beneath their feet.

❀ *Italian Prisoner of War*

U.S.A., 1946

He had brought more the feeling of soil than of weapons in his hands
and transported to the enemy's land he had come
much as a child might come.
Others, holding steel in their hearts, had travelled straight
to America. He, without wounds,
found Italy in the hills and flowers.

Nobody beat him. Through the wavering lengths of light and sun
he discovered the soil rich, his position certain.
Olives and oranges were his own home
and lilies of flowering paper in the dust
were familiar to him as the names of saints.

Until the shining car streaked through the gates
drew up beside him where he knelt and two
coloured photographs of girls leaned out and threw
gibberish at him like a pelt of stones,
then stopped and lanced his armband with their eyes,
he was secure.

But now, this surely was America.
Very foreign and strange and faraway.
The place his cousins went to like a myth
a bag apiece and garlanded with goodbyes
and had never been heard of since.

Now he was alien, without a tongue.
The hills tilted and were new, the crazy flowers
whispered and connived among themselves.
The armband wept on his arm,
he had become
alone in a grey landscape
where the sun
sputtered and dimmed and was no longer warm.

❀ *Old Man*

Brought to earth – the runner with souvenirs.
Slowed to a standstill in a northern garden
he remembers the lazy houseboat at Kashmir,
tulips on the roofs of the public buildings,
the caravan in Germany,
girl in a trance
and the pony-cart he drove on the roads of France.

Now in his green-legged trousers and here where
he had never wished to be, in this new, this north
land with a foreign people he cannot know
he walks the wild bewildering woods alone
wearing a sweater
found a decade ago
high up among the gentians near the snow.

Read classics as a boy. At fifty threw
the blue and golden volumes from his room
in a hotel in Venice one clear noon.
Changed to detective tales of death by-passed
and certain comics –
Batman, Superman
which prove the last shall surely be the first.

Always he had loved the flowers and now for his eyes
camas lilies – Mary-blue – and gorse,
its sweetness on the air by the water; flowers,
a picnic of them – fritillary, Indian's purse –
better when picked
held in his ancient hand
than growing from a strange and foreign earth.

But now, war ending, exiled among winds
and too-familiar servants, he desires
Europe and yesterday – and the flowers pale
before his paling eyes and the vivid grass
fades to a wash.
He hates this pallid place
and dreams a bright green future in the past.

❀ *Unable to Hate or Love*

In sight of land, everything came at him sharp and bright –
gulls suddener and a higher light on the wave.
New seeing made him a stranger to himself
and now, no longer one of the boys, he was quite alone
and lost in the larger body he had grown
during the sea trip; found himself shy
even with friends and nervous about the soil.

When the carrier came to dock he stood on deck
close-pressed among the rest. From the waiting bus
there to despatch him to a camp, he was
identical with the others – a khaki boy
released to freedom, returning from the East.
And though he had longed for freedom, found it hard
to visualize the walk along the street
or conversing with a girl
or the girl's speech.

It was almost as if there were figures behind his eyes
that he couldn't completely see around or through;
as if in front of him there were others who
partially blocked his view, who might even speak
gibberish or cry if he opened his mouth.

He wished, for the moment, he needn't go ashore
into this unknown city of friends. Already
the mayor had welcomed them by radio,
the sirens that hooted and screamed had made him a fool,
the people lining the docks were weeping for him
and everywhere hankies and flags fluttered but he
came from an unnamed country.

Three years he had dreamed this moment and how, running
he would tear with his smile the texture of this air;
he had dreamed that peace could instantly replace war.
But now he was home and about to land and he feared
the too-big spaces and the too-blue skies
and knew, at last, that most of his dreams were lies
and himself a prisoner still behind his face,
unable to be free in any place;
to hate the enemy as they wished him to
or love his countrymen as he would like to do.

Melanie's Nite-Book

❀ *Melanie's Nite-Book*

Note
I am not Melanie.
We do not know one another.
Yet her poems found among my papers paint
the underside of something I have known –
a parallel existence in a key
significantly lower.

They have their place
strike their own note, distort, darken
the belling
light.

Mother
She said I gave her her jewelled breasts
and he, my father, her jewelled pubis
In return, she gave me a diamond heart
a splinter of ice for either eye

In this family potlatch I want no part
I am giving her back her diamond heart

Sister

Sister little idiot one
whom I loved
and who loved me
like a plant perhaps
or bird
tamed by kindness
set apart
from another planet
where
other laws prevail
and who
barely entered
in this race

part of me
O part of me

Father

Father, O farther
in what heaven circlest thou?
Daily and dearly
ask I for thy succor

I see thee now
the red crease on thy brow
left where thy cap had rested
Crested ring
Buttons of brightest brass
High boots' high shine
dusty with pollen

from the flowering grass
of that unrolling upland
whose sweet air
was black and white
with magpies' flight
rank sweat of thy black horse

Father, O farther
forcest thou me to range
world-wide world over
searching evermore
obedient, house-trained
heel-trained, at thy call?

Who settest the world on fire
for others quenched
my smallest fire
uncoiled its acrid smoke
Whose flute thou lettest
others hear, whose drum …
My silence only
golden in thine ear

Father, O father
tremblest thou with dread
of my grey gaze
the twin of thy grey gaze?
I small, large-eyed
crunched in a tiny space
awaiting thy benediction
thy hand upon my head

Father, O father
cravest thou my grace?
Cravest forgiveness
for thy just rebukes
as I still crave thy praise

striving for thy approval
to appear
beautiful in thine eyes
or talented?

Father, father
can we call a truce?
Our binary stardom cancel
you from me
set free after how long –
two lifetimes? three? –
by that one word
which severs as it heals

Let me your spokesman
and your axeman be

Brother
You wore the looks I longed for
almond eyes
black from our gypsy forebears
milky skin
The creamy manner of your expensive school
lay sleek upon you
I was thin
acned and angular
No 'pretty girl'

Dreamed you displayed me
like a football trophy
took me to stag rock sessions
hockey games
places where I could loose
my female trace
my faint unearthly scent
my moon-pale face
Your slim twin sister
beautiful as Euclid

For it was written
All the ordered atoms
in orderly heaven
had ordained it so
And we obeyed that order
like a team
of harnessed horses driven
by skilled compassionate hands
or like a pair
of eagles riding
transparent muscles of air

Wakened to your abuse
the pale grey mornings
broke day after day
littered my room
your inkblots
on my notebooks
my stamps missing
no honey in the comb

Invented heroes to protect
young men
with fatal wounds
or dark congenital scars
White-meat invisible princes
sapphire-eyed
crippled
tubercular
Incurable invalids
who found me sweet as myrrh

These my companions
as I rode the subway
or climbed the interminable
steps to school
my co-conspirators
who let me love them
whom I called 'brother'
all my sister years

Ancestors
The cavernous theatre filled with them,
going back
generation on generation,
dressed in the colours of power:
scarlet and purple and black,
plumed and surpliced and gowned.
Men with arrogant Roman faces,
women like thoroughbred horses
held in check.

These were the people for whom
I had lived in exemplary fashion,
had not let down,
for whom I'd refrained from evil,
borne pain with grace.
And now they were here – resurrected –
the damned demanding dead,
jamming a theatre like head-cheese,
smelling of mothballs and scent,
brilliantine, shoe polish, Brasso
and old brocade.

Row after row
and tier after tier they ranged,
crowded together like eels
in the orchestra pit,
squeezed in the quilted boxes
and blocking the aisles
while I, on the stage alone,
last of the line,
pinned by the nails of their eyes,
was expected to give an account.

But the gypsies came in the nick
and flung themselves about.
They stamped their naked feet
dark with the dust of Spain,
clattered their castanets,
rattled their tambourines,
brandished their flashing knives
and put the lot to rout.

The Child

I dreamed the child was dead
and folded in a box
like stockings or a dress.

I dreamed its toys and games
its brightly coloured clothes
were lying on the grass

and with them I was left
adult and dutiful
with ink instead of blood.

I could not bear the grief
accommodate the loss –
as if my heart had died.

On wakening I saw
the child beside my bed
Not dead! not dead! I cried.

But startled by my voice
and fearful of my glance
the phantom infant fled.

Message

Not enough food

No drop of milk
No crumb

Only canned tongue

The Trail of Bread

What little the birds had overlooked
I found –
a first few meagre crumbs that led me on
from dark to darkest,
then the trail grew clear,
for deep in the airless wood
not even birds
ventured,
not enough sun,
no space to spread
their impeccable feathered arms.
(My wings were plucked.
Pin-feathers here and there.)

Whatever small rodents overlooked
I ate.
A skimpy nourishment.
It hurt my eyes
this meticulous search for food.
I might have stopped –
'stoppered', the word I want,
comparative,
a bottle sealed
inert, inanimate,
unable to move or open of itself.
(*I* could not move.
It moved me, opened me.)

Whatever they dropped for me
was miraculous,
multiple-purpose – food and way in one,
wakening me from nightmare,
leading on
out of that shadowy landscape
into dawn.

Rose of the air unfolding,
petal and thorn.
(A pencil sketch
with pale transparent wash –
watercolour on rice paper,
a wide brush.)
And sun, up with a rush.

The world gold-leafed and burnished:
gilded trees,
leaves like a jeweller's handwork,
grasses, ferns
filigreed and enamelled – Byzantine.
Cresses in clusters, bunched
beside a stream –
a glittering gold chain,
gold mesh, gold sheen,
where I bent down to drink.
(What birds then sang?)
Gold water in my mouth,
gold of my dreams
slipping like sovereigns
through my gold-rinsed hands.

Evening Dance of the Grey Flies

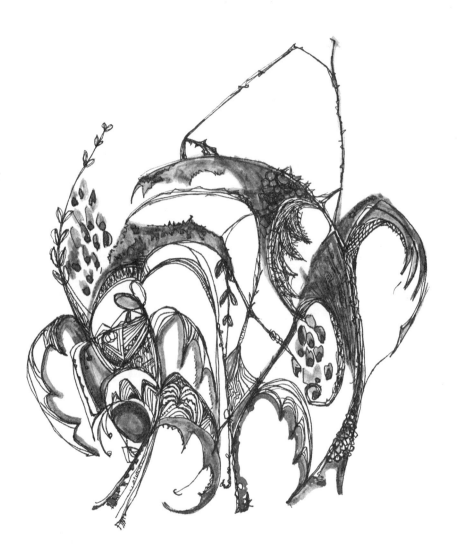

(i)

❈ Traveller's Palm

Miraculously plaited tree.
A sailor's knot
rooted,
a growing fan
whose grooved and slanted branches
are aqueducts
end-stopped
for tropical rains.

Knot, fan,
Quixote's windmill,
what-you-will –
for me, traveller,
a well.

On a hot day I took
a sharp and pointed knife,
plunged,
and water gushed
to my cupped mouth

old water
tasting green,
of vegetation and dust,
old water, warm as tears.

And in that tasting,
taster, water, air,
in temperature identical
were so
intricately merged
a fabulous foreign bird
flew silent from a void

lodged in my boughs.

❀ Finches Feeding

They fall like feathered cones from the tree above,
sumi the painted grass where the birdseed is,
skirl like a boiling pot
or a shallow within a river –
a bar of gravel breaking the water up.

Having said that, what have I said?
Not much.

Neither my delight nor the length of my watching is conveyed
and nothing profound recorded, yet these birds
as I observe them
stir such feelings up –
such yearnings for weightlessness, for hollow bones,
rapider heartbeat, east/west eyes
and such wonder – seemingly half remembered – as they rise
spontaneously into air, like feathered cones.

❀ *The Flower Bed*

Circular –
at a guess, twelve feet across –
and filled with a forest of sunflowers.
Girasoles turned sunward, yellow-lashed
black eyes staring at the sailing Sun.
No prospect of a blink
no fall or shift,
the focus constant, eye to eye engaged
as human eye can lock with human eye
and find within its ever-widening core,
such vastnesses of space
one's whole self tumbles in.

I see it in a glass or through a port,
crystalline,
refracting, like a globe,
its edges bending, sides distorted,
shine
of a thick lens,
the peep-hole through a door in which I *saw*
a tiny man
but *see* a bed of flowers
as bright as if enamelled yellow and green,
shooting their eye-beams at their Lord the Sun,
like so much spider's silk stretched true and taut.

And my own yellow eye, black lashed, provides
triangulation. We enmesh
three worlds with our geometry.
I learn,
in timeless Time at their green leafy school,
such silks and stares
such near-invisible straight curving lines
curving like Space itself
which merge and cross at the Omega point
and double back
to make transparent, multifoliate
Flowers of the Upper Air.

❀ *Short Spring Poem for the Short-Sighted*

Arabis
clotted cream
in the rockery

Framed by shrubs'
differing greens
the daffodils:
softgolden stars on stilts

Jonquils
red-eyed as vireos
peer out

And all the trees are clouds
pink clouds   or white
anchored by rusty hawsers

clouds of green
busy and airy
as a swarm of gnats

Soon now
the squeaky tulips
will cry 'O'

and 'O'

❀ Out Here: Flowering

> I have not been a tree long enough yet.
>
> JONATHAN GRIFFIN

Such stern weather. Metallic. When I was a human child
my surrogate mother smiled like that –
frostily from stone eyes – no heart in it –
a withering blasted cold
that coated me with ice – I, a small tree glistening in a field
of glassy snow – shot
beautifully through with rainbows and somehow – absolute.
But spoiled. Utterly spoiled.

No wonder the blossoming has been slow,
the springs like flares, the crowding flowers
a surfeit of whipped cream. How many years have I stood sere
brown and unseasonable in the subliming air?
But now the melt has begun and the weather pours
over me in a pelt of a petalled snow.

❃ Domestic Poem for a Summer Afternoon

The yellow garden-chair is newly webbed.
There, Arthur, full-length, reads of 'Toronto the Golden',
dozes, nods, lets fall his magazine.
From a golden book I read of Arthur, the King,
and Taliessen, the King's poet. I dream of the crown.
Was it jewelled with rubies, emeralds, stones the colour of his eyes?

The ducks are within arm's reach as usual
at this time in the afternoon – two mallards, webbed
feet tucked out of sight, they float
in unreflecting emerald grass. They doze.
Might be decoys, these wild water birds
unmoving as wood.

It is hot. Siesta still.
Not hot enough for Brazil but I think of Brazil
and the small yellow bird that flew in and perched
on the toe of Arthur's crossed-over foot,
puffed out its feathers, settled down for the night;
and the hummingbird, ruby-throated, a glowing coal
with the noise of a jet
that landed cool and light on the crown of his head.

We are settled down for the afternoon,
with whispering sprinklers and whirring jets.
We are so motionless we might be decoys
placed here by higher hunters who watch from their blind.
Arthur asleep has the face of a boy.
Like blue obsidian the drake's head glints.
His mate and I are brown in feather and skin
and above us the midsummer sun, crown of the sky,
shines indiscriminate down on duck and man.

❈ *Conchita Knows Who Who Is*

Quien sabe, Señora? Quien sabe?
    Conchita speaks.
Who broke the plate, Conchita?
Quien sabe, Señora?
What day of the week?
Who knows?
What time of day?
Quien sabe? Quien sabe, Señora?
    Boredom. Despair. Evasion.
    Shades of unknowing.
Where is the key?
Conchita, whose shoes are these?
Quien sabe, Señora? Quien sabe.
Who knows? Who knows.

    Who knows.
    A statement of fact.
    Of faith.
    WHO knows.
    Who knows who is this WHO?
    Conchita knows.
    Conchita knows WHO knows who broke the plate,
    what day, what hour, who stands beside the gate
    and where the key, and whose the shoes …
    Conchita knows who WHO is,
    one vast WHO
    in whom all questions are resolved
    all answers hiding.

Quien sabe, Señora. Quien sabe.
    Indulgent. Wise.
    Don't worry *your* head about it, child.
    WHO knows.

❈ Cullen Revisited

Cullen at fifty, arsonist, set fire
to the whole accumulation. Rings, wrongs, rights
from buds of flame burst into flower,
burned like magnesium – white – or red as rags.
The bag of tricks banged off – flared, fumed, smoked.
Butt ends of jokes, lexicons, old chains like briars
glowed in the night sky. Strange constellations rose.
The conflagration could be seen for miles.

Cullen among the charred remains – himself
down to the bone – scuffed, shuffled, poked.
Recognized nothing. The span of his life reduced
to nails, pearl buttons, gravel, twists of wire –
all hard, all black, all useless. Cullen smiled
and a wind arose like the wind the Holy Ghost
bears in its wings – and the flames broke out and smoked
and flickered in white and gold before they died
for the second time in a feathery ash as grey
and soft as feathers plucked from a dove.

Cullen, departing, stubbed his toe, upturned
(darkened face of the moon at solar eclipse)
a disc, heart-sized and heavy for its size.
Makeweight, touchstone, lodestar. And this he kept.
It squinted where he rubbed it.
Like an eye.

So Cullen began again. Trees bloomed. Sun shone.
And he, the Ace of Wands, green-sprigged, was borne
high in a Giant Hand through a running sky.
At night in a rain of shooting stars, he slept.
The heart as a Rose, Imperial palms – and jewels
from an underground cavern filled his head.

Veins on fire, he dreamed the grey days through
like a wintering bear. He waked
to tea-coloured kings and queens upright as staves –
small, wren-boned, walking in purple, heads
bound in embroideries, braceleted wrists –
and all reflected as though in water, twinned
like royalty in a card deck.
                                        Cullen slept
and tall, black, naked warriors like divs
sprang from the earth like grain – green at the groin –
constructed walls of intricate mosaics,
each stone polished and cut and then exactly placed.
As Cullen waked, the sly disc winked and shone.

All this was in World One.
                                        World Two was where
he explored the golden ship – cabins and hold –
hoisted its golden sails and from its gold
crow's-nest sighted – Third World …
hazy at first, and seen from his position,
halfway between earth and heaven,
half blinded by the sun,
seeming to rock.
                    And hum.

❁ *For Mstislav Rostropovich with Love*

Listening ear
a conduit for these sounds,
I watch your bowing arm
and see beneath
your sleeve, shirtcuff
and pliant sheath of skin,
a wrist of stainless steel
precision-turned,
fluid with bearings,
bright as adamant
with power to blind us
like a silver sun;
while gazing fearless
fire into fire
the enduring pupil
of my inner eye
made in the manner
that you made your wrist –
of matter primal and alchemical
impervious to accident
or hurt.

This is already much.
But there is more:
what falls apart is held together
each
atom aligned
and in its proper place.
So great an order interlocks my flesh
that I, as centred
as a spinning top
am perfectly asleep
(which, in this sense
means, if not *perfectly*
then *more* awake).

And as an atom –
one among these rapt
like-centred listeners –
I am part
of that essential
intricate design
which forms a larger unit –
mutable
around its sleeping core –
while it, in turn,
part of a vaster
one I barely glimpse –
already cosmic –
leads us to the stars.

Maestro, *salud*.
Perfection in an art
can heal an open wound,
a broken heart
or fuse fragmented man.

Tonight, are we not proof?

❁ *Motel Pool*

The plump good-natured children play in the blue pool:
roll and plop; plop and roll;

slide and tumble, oiled, in the slippery sun
silent as otters, turning over and in,

churning the water; or – seamstresses – cut and sew
with jackknives its satins invisibly.

Not beautiful, but suddenly limned with light
their elliptical wet flesh in a flash reflects it

and it greens the green grass, greens the hanging leaf
greens Adam and Eden, greens little Eve.

❀ *Stefan*

Stefan
aged eleven
looked at the baby and said
When he thinks it must be pure thought
because he hasn't any words yet
and we
proud parents
admiring friends
who had looked at the baby

looked at the baby again

✽ Ecology

If a boy
eats an apple
because a bee
collects nectar,
what happens
because a boy
eats an apple?

(ii)

❀ *Phone Call from Mexico*

Over the years and miles   your
voice   weeping
telling me you are old
have lost your mind
and all the winds and waters of
America
sound in your words

I see your house
a square-cut topaz   set
within a larger   square
tangle of garden
walled
Brick walks
wild dahlias
raspberry canes and dogs
Raised ladies' flowerbeds
crammed with mignonettes
lobelias
little red-eyes
all the buzz
and hum of summer

It is hot
The golden sun rains down
its golden dust
upon you   shrunken
toothless   lonely   I
do not know this
person
Elinor
Don't know   can't see
you as you say you are
a shrivelled pod
rattling   rasping
a crazed creature
dazed
butting the golden air
with your goat's head
crying against
your gods your gods your gods
whom once you sensed
benign caretakers of
the realms   dominions of
your provenance
and now know baneful
black   obsidian
to be confronted
and destroyed

How tell you they
are ungods
Elinor?
How urge you to unlock
and put aside
your clumsy armour
manic armaments
and impotent blind rage?
to lay your head
down gently
like a quarrelsome
tired child?
A phone call
will not do
cannot give comfort   can
not thorns extract
nor antidote
force down
Over this distance
cannot touch your hand

Your voice is broken arrows
You are all
those whom I love
who age ungainly
whose
joints   hearts   psyches
minds   unhinge
and whom
I cannot mend
or ease

How do we end
this phone call
Elinor?
You
railing and roiling
over miles and years
And I
in tears

❀ *Custodian*

I watch it.
Lock and stock.
No joke.
It is my job.

I dust, I wash, I guard
this fading fibre;
polish even.
Spit.

And rub I it
and shine
and wear it to the bone.
Lay bare its nub.

It is but matter
and it matters not
one whit or tittle
if I wear it out.

Yet mend I it and darn
and patch
and pat it even
like a dog

that which the Auctioneer
when I am gone,
for nearly nought
will knock down
from his block.

✻ *Fly: On Webs*

Two kinds of web: the one
not there. A sheet of glass.
Look! I am flying through air,
spinning in emptiness ... SPUNG!
... bounced on a flexible wire,
caught by invisible guys.

The other a filigree, gold
as the call of a trumpet. A sun
to my myriad-faceted eye.
A season. A climate. Compelled
and singing hosannas I fly:
I dazzle. I struggle. I drown.

❀ *About Death*

I.
And at the moment of death
what is correct procedure?

Cut the umbilical, they said.

And with the umbilical cut
how then prepare the body?

Wash it in sacred water.
Dress it in silk for the wedding.

2.
I wash and iron for you
your final clothes
(my heart on your sleeve)
wishing to wash your flesh
wishing to close
your sightless eyes

nothing remains to do

I am a vacant house

✾ A Grave Illness

Someone was shovelling gravel all that week.
The flowering plums came out.
Rose-coloured streets
branched in my head –
spokes of a static wheel
spinning and whirring only when I coughed.
And sometimes, afterwards, I couldn't tell
if I had coughed or he had shovelled. Which.

Someone was shovelling until it hurt.
The rasp of metal on cement, the scrape
and fall
of all that broken rock.
Such industry day after day. For what?
My cough's accompanist?
The flowering trees
blossomed behind my eyes in drifts of red
delicate petals. I was hot.
The shovel grated in my breaking chest.

Someone was shovelling gravel. Was it I?
Burying me in shifts and shards of rock
up to my gasping throat. My head was out
dismembered, sunken-eyed
as John the Baptist's on a plate.
Meanwhile the plum
blossoms trickling from above
through unresistant air
fell on my eyes and hair
as crimson as my blood.

❀ *Ours*

For Patrick Anderson – d. 1979

At something over sixty he is dead
and I, a friend of his twenties,
I am still – tentatively – here.

'Friend'. Were we friends?
Our alliance something less:
acquaintances who knew each other well
and met each other often,
warmed by the same blaze.

Sparked by his singular talent
my small fires
angered him.

He wished me near,
appreciative of his skills,
aficionada of good writing.
His good writing.
Not to write well.

Hard to be friends.
Ditches and hedges between.
And yet, at times
our hearts both leapt
in love with metaphor,
or we laughed, played verbal handball,
eyes locked. We were friends.

Now he is dead.
And I think of the breath
he breathed into his poems
and of how
with nothing passing for love between us
something passed
something memorable and alive –

a kind of walking bird
which, when we least expected,
would suddenly take flight.

His and mine, that bird. Ours.
Now
unable to fly.

❀ Voyager

At the age at which he died and within
days of that date
I lie outstretched
the robins listening on the grass
and the cerise
rhododendron levitating in a far
part of the garden –
                             I, with my life
half over – *spent* – yet still
dreaming of him. My father.

He comes back
night after night
from some long journey
reluctant to return
bored to be home, disregarding our
presence, acting as if
we were not there –
a blank space in the air –
or seeing us and passing us by with no
glance of recognition.

And we always so eager,
welcoming each time, pleased
at his safe return
glad at the sight of
his face.

Last night
he returned again
companions with him from some long
inter-galactic voyage
and his friends spoke to us,

asked who we were but he
sought us in other places
studied maps,
set out in search.

It was the closest we have come
to meeting
during thirty years of dreams.

❈ *Evening Dance of the Grey Flies*

Grey flies, fragile, slender-winged and slender-legged
scribble a pencilled script across the sunlit lawn.

As grass and leaves grow black
the grey flies gleam –
their cursive flight a gold calligraphy.

It is the light that gilds their frail
bodies, makes them fat and bright as bees –
reflected or refracted light –

as once my fist
burnished by some beam I could not see
glowed like gold mail and conjured Charlemagne

as once your face
grey with illness and with age –
a silverpoint against the pillow's white –

shone suddenly like the sun
before you died.

(iii)

❀ Unless the Eye Catch Fire ...

Unless the eye catch fire
  The God will not be seen ...
      Where the Wasteland Ends, THEODORE ROSZAK

Wednesday, September 17. The day began normally enough. The quails, cockaded as antique foot soldiers, arrived while I was having my breakfast. The males black-faced, white-necklaced, cinnamon-crowned, with short, sharp, dark plumes. Square bibs, Payne's grey; belly and sides with a pattern of small stitches. Reassuring, the flock of them. They tell me the macadamization of the world is not complete.

A sudden alarm, and as if they had one brain among them, they were gone in a rush – a sideways ascending Niagara – shutting out the light, obscuring the sky and exposing a rectangle of lawn, unexpectedly emerald. How bright the berries on the cotoneaster. Random leaves on the cherry twirled like gold spinners. The garden was high-keyed, vivid, locked in aspic.

Without warning, and as if I were looking down the tube of a kaleidoscope, the merest shake occurred – moiréed the garden – rectified itself. Or, more precisely, as if a range-finder through which I had been sighting found of itself a more accurate focus. Sharpened, in fact, to an excoriating exactness.

And then the colours changed. Shifted to a higher octave – a *bright spectrum*. Each colour with its own *light*, its own *shape*. The leaves of the trees, the berries, the grasses – as if shedding successive films – disclosed layer after layer of hidden perfections. And upon these rapidly changing surfaces the 'range-finder' – to really play hob with metaphor! – sharpened its small invisible blades.

I don't know how to describe the intensity and speed of focus of this gratuitous zoom lens through which I stared, or the swift and dizzying adjustments within me. I became a 'sleeping top,' perfectly centred, perfectly sighted. The colours vibrated beyond the visible range of the spectrum. Yet I saw them. With some matching eye. Whole galaxies of them, blazing and glowing, flowing in rivulets, gushing in fountains – volatile, mercurial, and making lacklustre and off-key the colours of the rainbow.

I had no time or inclination to wonder, intellectualize. My mind seemed astonishingly clear and quite still. Like a crystal. A burning glass.

And then the range-finder sharpened once again. To alter space.

The lawn, the bushes, the trees – still super-brilliant – were no longer *there*. *There*, in fact, had ceased to exist. They were now, of all places in the world, *here*. Right in the centre of my being. Occupying an immense inner space. Part of me. Mine. Except the whole idea of ownership was beside the point. As true to say I was theirs as they mine. I and they were here; they and I, there. (*There, here* ... odd ... but for an irrelevant, inconsequential 't' which comes and goes, the words are the same.)

As suddenly as the world had altered, it returned to normal. I looked at my watch. A ridiculous mechanical habit. As I had no idea when the experience began it was impossible to know how long it had lasted. What had seemed eternity couldn't have been more than a minute or so. My coffee was still steaming in its mug.

The garden, through the window, was as it had always been. Yet not as it had always been. Less. Like listening to mono after hearing stereo. But with a far greater loss of dimension. A grievous loss.

I rubbed my eyes. Wondered, not without alarm, if this was the onset of some disease of the retina – glaucoma or some cellular change in the eye itself – superlatively packaged, fatally sweet as the marzipan cherry I ate as a child and *knew* was poison.

If it *is* a disease, the symptoms will recur. It will happen again.

Tuesday, September 23. It *has* happened again.

Tonight, taking Dexter for his late walk, I looked up at the crocheted tangle of boughs against the sky. Dark silhouettes against the lesser dark, but beating now with an extraordinary black brilliance. The golden glints in obsidian or the lurking embers in black opals are the nearest I can come to describing them. But it's a false description, emphasizing as it does the wrong end of the scale. This was a *dark spectrum*. As if the starry heavens were translated into densities of black – black Mars, black Saturn, black Jupiter; or a master jeweller had crossed his jewels with jet and set them to burn and wink in the branches and twigs of oaks whose leaves shone luminous – a leafy Milky Way – fired by black chlorophyll.

Dexter stopped as dead as I. Transfixed. His thick honey-coloured coat and amber eyes, glowing with their own intense brightness, suggested yet another spectrum. A *spectrum of light*. He was a constellated dog, shining, supra-real, against the foothills and mountain ranges of midnight.

I am reminded now, as I write, of a collection of lepidoptera in Brazil – one entire wall covered with butterflies, creatures of daylight – enormous or tiny – blue, orange, black. Strong-coloured. And on the opposite wall their antiselves – pale night flyers spanning such a range of silver and white and lightest snuff-colour that once one entered their spectral scale there was no end to the subleties and delicate nuances. But I didn't think like this then. All thought, all comparisons were prevented by the startling infinities of darkness and light.

Then, as before, the additional shake occurred and the two spectrums moved swiftly from without to within. As if two equal and complementary circles centred inside me – or I in them. How explain that I not only *saw* but actually *was* the two spectrums? (I underline a simple, but in this case exactly appropriate, anagram.)

Then the range-finder lost its focus and the world, once again, was back to normal. Dexter, a pale, blurred blob, bounded about within the field of my peripheral vision, going on with his doggy interests just as if a moment before he had not been frozen in his tracks, a dog entranced.

I am no longer concerned about my eyesight. Wonder only if we are both mad, Dexter and I? Angelically mad, sharing hallucinations of epiphany. *Folie à deux?*

Friday, October 3. It's hard to account for my secrecy, for I *have* been secretive. As if the cat had my tongue. It's not that I don't long to talk about the colours but I can't risk the wrong response – (as Gaby once said of a companion after a faultless performance of *Giselle*: 'If she had criticized the least detail of it, I'd have hit her!').

Once or twice I've gone so far as to say, 'I had the most extraordinary experience the other day ...' hoping to find some look or phrase, some answering, 'So did I.' None has been forthcoming.

I can't forget the beauty. Can't get it out of my head. Startling, unearthly, indescribable. Infuriatingly indescribable. A glimpse of – somewhere else. Somewhere alive, miraculous, newly made yet timeless. And more important still – significant, luminous, with a meaning of which I was part. Except that I – the I who is writing this – did not exist: was flooded out, dissolved in that immensity where subject and object are one.

I have to make a deliberate effort now not to live my life in terms of it; not to sit, immobilized, awaiting the shake that heralds a new world. Awaiting the transfiguration.

Luckily the necessities of life keep me busy. But upstream of my actions, behind a kind of plate glass, some part of me waits, listens, maintains a total attention.

Tuesday, October 7. Things are moving very fast.

Some nights ago my eye was caught by a news item. 'Trucker Blames Colours,' went the headline. Reading on: 'R.T. Ballantyne, driver for Island Trucks, failed to stop on a red light at the intersection of Fernhill and Spender. Questioned by traffic police, Ballantyne replied: "I didn't see it, that's all. There was this shake, then all these colours suddenly in the trees. Real bright ones I'd never seen before. I guess they must have blinded me." A breathalyzer test proved negative.' Full stop.

I had an overpowering desire to talk to R.T. Ballantyne. Even looked him up in the telephone book. Not listed. I debated reaching him through Island Trucks in the morning.

Hoping for some mention of the story, I switched on the local radio station, caught the announcer mid-sentence:

'… to come to the studio and talk to us. So far no one has been able to describe just what the "new" colours are, but perhaps Ruby Howard can. Ruby, you say you actually *saw* "new" colours?'

What might have been a flat, rather ordinary female voice was sharpened by wonder. 'I was out in the garden, putting it to bed, you might say, getting it ready for winter. The hydrangeas are dried out – you know the way they go. Soft beiges and greys. And I was thinking maybe I should cut them back, when there was this – shake, like – and there they were shining. Pink. And blue. But not like they are in life. Different. Brighter. With little lights, like …'

The announcer's voice cut in, 'You say "not like they are in life". D'you think this wasn't life? I mean, do you think maybe you were dreaming?'

'Oh, no,' answered my good Mrs Howard, positive, clear, totally unrattled. 'Oh, no, I wasn't *dreaming*. Not *dreaming* – ... Why – *this* is more like dreaming.' She was quiet a moment and then, in a matter-of-fact voice, 'I can't expect you to believe it,' she said. 'Why should you? I wouldn't believe it myself if I hadn't seen it.' Her voice expressed a kind of compassion as if she was really sorry for the announcer.

I picked up the telephone book for the second time, looked up the number of the station. I had decided to tell Mrs Howard what I had seen. I dialled, got a busy signal, depressed the bar and waited, cradle in hand. I dialled again. And again.

Later. J. just phoned. Curious how she and I play the same game over and over.

J: Were you watching Channel 8?

ME: No, I ...

J: An interview. With a lunatic. One who sees colours and flashing lights.

ME: Tell me about it.

J: He was a logger – a high-rigger – not that that has anything to do with it. He's retired now and lives in an apartment and has a window-box with geraniums. This morning the flowers were like neon, he said, flashing and shining ... *Honestly!*

ME: Perhaps he saw something you can't ...

J: (*Amused*) I might have known you'd take his side. Seriously, what *could* he have seen?

ME: Flashing and shining – as he said.

J: But they couldn't. Not geraniums. And you know it as well as I do. *Honestly*, Babe ... (She is the only person left who calls me the name my mother called me.) Why are you always so perverse?

I felt faithless. I put down the receiver, as if I had not borne witness to my God.

October 22. Floods of letters to the papers. Endless interviews on radio and TV. Pros, cons, inevitable spoofs.

One develops an eye for authenticity. It's as easy to spot as sunlight. However they may vary in detail, true accounts of the colours have an unmistakable common factor – a common factor as difficult to convey as sweetness to those who know only salt. True accounts are inarticulate, diffuse, unlikely – impossible.

It's recently crossed my mind that there may be some relationship between having seen the colours and their actual manifestation – something as improbable as *the more one sees them the more they are able to be seen.* Perhaps they are always there in some normally invisible part of the electro-magnetic spectrum and only become visible to certain people at certain times. A combination of circumstances or some subtle refinement in the organ of sight. And then – from quantity to quality perhaps, like water to ice – a whole community changes, is able to see, catches fire.

For example, it was seven days between the first time I saw the colours and the second. During that time there were no reports to the media. But once the reports began, the time between lessened appreciably *for me.* Not proof, of course, but worth noting. And I can't help wondering why some people see the colours and others don't. Do some of us have extra vision? Are some so conditioned that they're virtually blind to what's there before their very noses? Is it a question of more, or less?

Reports come in from farther and farther afield; from all walks of life. I think now there is no portion of the inhabited globe without 'shake freaks' and no acceptable reason for the sightings. Often, only one member of a family will testify to the heightened vision. In my own small circle, I am the only witness – or so I think. I feel curiously hypocritical as I listen to my friends denouncing the 'shakers'. Drugs, they say. Irrational – possibly dangerous. Although no sinister incidents have occurred yet – just some mild shake-baiting here and there – one is uneasily reminded of Salem.

Scientists pronounce us hallucinated or mistaken, pointing out that so far there is no hard evidence, no objective proof. That means, I suppose, no photographs, no spectroscopic measurement – if such is possible. Interestingly, seismographs show very minor earthquake tremors – showers of them, like shooting stars in August. Pundits claim 'shake fever' – as it has come to be called – is a variant on flying saucer fever and that it will subside in its own time. Beneficent physiologists suggest we are suffering (why is it *always* suffering, never enjoying?) a distorted form of *ocular spectrum* or after-image. (An after-image of what?) Psychologists disagree among themselves. All in all, it is not surprising that some of us prefer to keep our experiences to ourselves.

January 9. Something new has occurred. Something impossible. Disturbing. So disturbing, in fact, that according to rumour it is already being taken with the utmost seriousness at the highest levels. TV, press and radio – with good reason – talk of little else.

What seemingly began as a mild winter has assumed sinister overtones. Farmers in southern Alberta are claiming the earth is unnaturally hot to the touch. Golfers at Harrison complain that the soles of their feet burn. Here on the coast, we notice it less. Benign winters are our specialty.

Already we don't lack for explanations as to why the earth could not be hotter than usual, nor why it is naturally 'un-naturally' hot. Vague notes of reassurance creep into the speeches of public men. They may be unable to explain the issue, but they can no longer ignore it.

To confuse matters further, reports on temperatures seem curiously inconsistent. What information we get comes mainly from self-appointed 'earth touchers'. And now that the least thing can fire an argument, their conflicting readings lead often enough to inflammatory debate.

For myself, I can detect no change at all in my own garden.

Thursday...? There is no longer any doubt. The temperature of the earth's surface *is* increasing.

It is unnerving, horrible, to go out and feel the ground like some great beast, warm, beneath one's feet. As if another presence – vast, invisible – attends one. Dexter, too, is perplexed. He barks at the earth with the same indignation and, I suppose, fear, with which he barks at the first rumblings of earthquake.

Air temperatures, curiously, don't increase proportionately – or so we're told. It doesn't make sense, but at the moment nothing makes sense. Countless explanations have been offered. Elaborate explanations. None adequate. The fact that the air temperature remains temperate despite the higher ground heat must, I think, be helping to keep panic down. Even so, these are times of great tension.

Hard to understand these two unexplained – unrelated? – phenomena: the first capable of dividing families; the second menacing us all. We are like animals trapped in a burning building.

Later. J. just phoned. Terrified. Why don't I move in with her, she urges. After all she has the space and we have known each other forty years. (Hard to believe when I don't feel even forty!) She can't bear it – the loneliness.

Poor J. Always so protected, insulated by her money. And her charm. What one didn't provide, the other did … diversions, services, attention.

What do I think is responsible for the heat, she asks. But it turns out she means who. Her personal theory is that the 'shake-freaks' are causing it – involuntarily, perhaps, but the two are surely linked.

'How could they possibly cause it?' I enquire. 'By what reach of the imagination …?'

'Search *me!*' she protests. 'How on earth should *I* know?' And the sound of the dated slang makes me really laugh.

But suddenly she is close to tears. 'How can you *laugh?*' she calls. 'This is nightmare. Nightmare!'

Dear J. I wish I could help but the only comfort I could offer would terrify her still more.

September. Summer calmed us down. If the earth was hot, well, summers *are* hot. And we were simply having an abnormally hot one.

Now that it is fall – the season of cool nights, light frosts – and the earth like a feverish child remains worryingly hot, won't cool down, apprehension mounts.

At last we are given official readings. For months the authorities have assured us with irrefutable logic that the temperature of the earth could not be increasing. Now, without any apparent period of indecision or confusion, they are warning us with equal conviction and accurate statistical documentation that it has, in fact, increased. Something anyone with a pocket-handkerchief of lawn has known for some time.

Weather stations, science faculties, astronomical observatories all over the world are measuring and reporting. Intricate computerized tables are quoted. Special departments of Government have been set up. We speak now of a new Triassic Age – the Neo-Triassic – and of the accelerated melting of the ice caps. But we are elaborately assured that this could not, repeat not, occur in our lifetime.

Interpreters and analysts flourish. The media are filled with theories and explanations. The increased temperature has been attributed to impersonal agencies such as bacteria from outer space; a thinning of the earth's atmosphere; a build-up of carbon-dioxide in the air; some axial irregularity; a change in the earth's core (geologists are reported to have begun test borings). No theory is too far-fetched to have its supporters. And because man likes a scapegoat, blame has been laid upon NASA, atomic physicists, politicians, the occupants of flying saucers and finally upon mankind at large – improvident, greedy mankind – whose polluted, strike-ridden world is endangered now by the fabled flames of hell.

Yet, astonishingly, life goes on. The Pollack baby was born last week. I received the news as if it were a death. Nothing has brought the irony of our situation home to me so poignantly. And when I saw the perfect little creature in its mother's arms, the look of adoration on her face, I found myself saying the things one always says to a new mother – exactly as if the world had not changed. Exactly as if our radio was not informing us that Nostradamus, the Bible, and Jeane Dixon have all foreseen our plight. A new paperback, *Let Edgar Cayce Tell You Why* sold out in a matter of days. Attendance at churches has doubled. Cults proliferate. Yet even in this atmosphere, we, the 'shake freaks', are considered lunatic fringe. Odd men out. In certain quarters I believe we are seriously held responsible for the escalating heat, so J. is not alone. There have now been one or two nasty incidents. It is not surprising that even the most vocal among us have grown less willing to talk. I am glad to have kept silent. As a woman living alone, the less I draw attention to myself the better.

But, at the same time, we have suddenly all become neighbours. Total strangers greet each other on the street. And the almost invisible couple behind the high hedge appears every time I pass with Dexter – wanting to talk. Desperately wanting to talk.

For our lives are greatly altered by this overhanging sense of doom. It is already hard to buy certain commodities. Dairy products are in very short supply. On the other hand, the market is flooded with citrus fruits. We are threatened with severe shortages for the future. The authorities are resisting rationing but it will have to come, if only to prevent artificial shortages resulting from hoarding.

Luckily the colours are an almost daily event. I see them now, as it were, with my entire being. It is as if all my cells respond to their brilliance and become light too. At such times I feel I might shine in the dark.

No idea of the date. It is evening and I am tired but I am so far behind in my notes I want to get something down. Events have moved too fast for me.

Gardens, parks – every tillable inch of soil – have been appropriated for food crops. As an able, if aging body, with an acre of land and some knowledge of gardening, I have been made responsible for soybeans – small trifoliate plants rich with the promise of protein. Neat rows of them cover what were once my vegetable garden, flower beds, lawn.

Young men from the Department of Agriculture came last month, bulldozed, cultivated, planted. Efficient, noisy desecrators of my twenty years of landscaping. Dexter barked at them from the moment they appeared and I admit I would have shared his indignation had the water shortage not already created its own desolation.

As a Government gardener I'm a member of a new privileged class. I have watering and driving permits and coupons for gasoline and boots – an indication of what is to come. So far there has been no clothes rationing.

Daily instructions – when to water and how much, details of mulching, spraying – reach me from the Government radio station to which I tune first thing in the morning. It also provides temperature readings, weather forecasts and the latest news releases on emergency measures, curfews, rationing, insulation. From the way things are going I think it will soon be our only station. I doubt that newspapers will be able to print much longer. In any event, I have already given them up. At first it was interesting to see how quickly drugs, pollution, education, women's lib., all became bygone issues; and, initially, I was fascinated to see how we rationalized. Then I became bored. Then disheartened. Now I am too busy.

Evening. A call came from J. Will I come for Christmas?

Christmas! Extraordinary thought. Like a word from another language learned in my youth, now forgotten.

'I've still got some Heidseck. We can get tight.'

The word takes me back to my teens. 'Like old times ...'

'Yes.' She is eager. I hate to let her down. 'J., I can't. How could I get to you?'

'In your *car*, silly. *You* still have gas. You're the only one of us who has.' Do I detect a slight hint of accusation, as if I had acquired it illegally?

'But J., it's only for emergencies.'

'My God, Babe, d'you think *this* isn't an emergency?'

'J., dear ...'

'*Please*, Babe,' she pleads. 'I'm so afraid. Of the looters. The eeriness. You must be afraid too. *Please!*'

I should have said, yes, that of course I was afraid. It's only natural to be afraid. Or, unable to say that, I should have made the soothing noises a mother makes to her child. Instead, 'There's no reason to be afraid, J.,' I said. It must have sounded insufferably pompous.

'No reason!' She was exasperated with me. 'I'd have thought there was every reason.'

She will phone again. In the night perhaps when she can't sleep. Poor J. She feels so alone. She *is* so alone. And so idle. I don't suppose it's occurred to her yet that telephones will soon go. That a whole way of life is vanishing completely.

It's different for me. I have the soybeans which keep me busy all the daylight hours. And Dexter. And above all I have the colours and with them the knowledge that there are others, other people, whose sensibilities I share. We are as invisibly, inviolably related to one another as the components of a molecule. I say 'we'. Perhaps I should speak only for myself, yet I feel as sure of these others as if they had spoken. Like the quails, we share one brain – no, I think it is one heart – between us. How do I know this? How *do* I know? I know by knowing. We are less alarmed by the increasing heat than those who have not seen the colours. I can't explain why. But seeing the colours seems to change one – just as certain diagnostic procedures cure the complaint they are attempting to diagnose.

In all honesty I admit to having had moments when this sense of community was not enough, when I have had a great longing for my own kind – for so have I come to think of these others – in the way one has a great longing for someone one loves. Their presence in the world is not enough. One must see them. Touch them. Speak with them.

But lately that longing has lessened. All longing, in fact. And fear. Even my once great dread that I might cease to see the colours has vanished. It is as if through seeing them I have learned to see them. Have learned to be ready to see – passive; not striving to see – active. It keeps me very wide awake. Transparent even. Still.

The colours come daily now. Dizzying. Transforming. Life-giving. My sometimes back-breaking toil in the garden is lightened, made full of wonder, by the incredible colours shooting in the manner of children's sparklers from the plants themselves and from my own work-worn hands. I hadn't realized that I too am part of this vibrating luminescence.

Later. I have no idea how long it is since I abandoned these notes. Without seasons to measure its passing, without normal activities – preparations for festivals, occasional outings – time feels longer, shorter or – more curious still – simultaneous, undifferentiated. Future and past fused in the present. Linearity broken.

I had intended to write regularly, but the soybeans keep me busy pretty well all day and by evening I'm usually ready for bed. I'm sorry however to have missed recording the day-by-day changes. They were more or less minor at first. But once the heat began its deadly escalation, the world as we have known it – 'our world' – had you been able to put it alongside 'this world' – would have seemed almost entirely different.

No one, I think, could have foreseen the speed with which everything has broken down. For instance, the elaborate plans made to maintain transportation became useless in a matter of months. Private traffic was first curtailed, then forbidden. If a man from another planet had looked in on us, he would have been astonished to see us trapped who were apparently free.

The big changes only really began after the first panic evacuations from the cities. Insulated by concrete, sewer pipes and underground parkades, high density areas responded slowly to the increasing temperatures. But once the heat penetrated their insulations, Gehennas were created overnight and whole populations fled in hysterical exodus, jamming highways in their futile attempts to escape.

Prior to this the Government had not publicly acknowledged a crisis situation. They had taken certain precautions, brought in temporary measures to ease shortages and dealt with new developments on an *ad hoc* basis. Endeavoured to play it cool. Or so it seemed. Now they levelled with us. It was obvious that they must have been planning for months, only awaiting the right psychological moment to take everything over. That moment had clearly come. What we had previously thought of as a free world ended. We could no longer eat, drink, move without permits or coupons. This was full-scale emergency.

Yet nothing proceeds logically. Plans are made only to be remade to accommodate new and totally unexpected developments. The heat, unpatterned as disseminated sclerosis, attacks first here, then there. Areas of high temperature suddenly and inexplicably cool off – or vice versa. Agronomists are doing everything possible to keep crops coming – taking advantage of hot-house conditions to force two crops where one had grown before – frantically playing a kind of agricultural roulette, gambling on the length of time a specific region might continue to grow temperate-zone produce.

Mails have long since stopped. And newspapers. And telephones. As a member of a new privileged class, I have been equipped with a two-way radio and a permit to drive on Government business. Schools have of course closed. An attempt was made for a time to provide lessons over TV. Thankfully the looting and rioting seem over. Those desperate gangs of angry citizens who for some time made life additionally difficult, have now disappeared. We seem at last to understand that we are all in this together.

Life is very simple without electricity. I get up with the light and go to bed as darkness falls. My food supply is still substantial and because of the soybean crop I am all right for water. Dexter has adapted well to his new life. He is outdoors less than he used to be and has switched to a mainly vegetable diet without too much difficulty.

Evening. This morning a new order over the radio. All of us with special driving privileges were asked to report to our zone garage to have our tires treated with heat-resistant plastic.

I had not been into town for months. I felt rather as one does on returning home from hospital – that the world is unexpectedly large, with voluminous airy spaces. This was exaggerated perhaps by the fact that our whole zone had been given over to soybeans. Everywhere the same rows of green plants – small pods already formed – march across gardens and boulevards. I was glad to see the climate prove so favourable. But there was little else to make me rejoice as I drove through ominously deserted streets, paint blistering and peeling on fences and houses, while overhead a haze of dust, now always with us, created a green sun.

The prolonged heat has made bleak the little park opposite the garage. A rocky little park, once all mosses and rhododendrons, it is bare now, and brown. I was seeing the day as everyone saw it. Untransmuted.

As I stepped out of my car to speak to the attendant I cursed that I had not brought my insulators. The burning tarmac made me shift rapidly from foot to foot. Anyone from another planet would have wondered at this extraordinary quirk of earthlings. But my feet were forgotten as my eyes alighted a second time on the park across the way. I had never before seen so dazzling and variegated a display of colours. How could there be such prismed brilliance in the range of greys and browns? It was as if the perceiving organ – wherever it is – sensitized by earlier experience, was now correctly tuned for this further perception.

The process was as before: the merest shake and the whole park was 'rainbow, rainbow, rainbow'. A further shake brought the park from *there* to *here*. Interior. But this time the interior space had increased. Doubled. By a kind of instant knowledge that rid me of all doubt, I knew that the garage attendant was seeing it too. *We saw the colours*.

Then, with that slight shift of focus, as if a gelatinous film had moved briefly across my sight, everything slipped back.

I really looked at the attendant for the first time. He was a skinny young man standing up naked inside a pair of loose striped overalls cut off at the knee, *sidney* embroidered in red over his left breast pocket. He was blond, small-boned, with nothing about him to stick in the memory except his clear eyes which at that moment bore an expression of total comprehension.

'You ...' we began together and laughed.

'Have you seen them before?' I asked. But it was rather as one would say 'how do you do' – not so much a question as a salutation.

We looked at each other for a long time, as if committing each other to memory.

'Do you know anyone else?' I said.

'One or two. Three, actually. Do you?'

I shook my head. 'You are the first. Is it ... is it ... always like that?'

'You mean ...?' he gestured towards his heart.

I nodded.

'Yes,' he said. 'Yes, it is.'

There didn't seem anything more to talk about. Your right hand hasn't much to say to your left, or one eye to the other. There was comfort in the experience, if comfort is the word, which it isn't. More as if an old faculty had been extended. Or a new one activated.

Sidney put my car on the hoist and sprayed its tires.

Some time later. I have not seen Sidney again. Two weeks ago when I went back he was not there and as of yesterday, cars have become obsolete. Not that we will use that word publicly. The official word is *suspended*.

Strange to be idle after months of hard labour. A lull only before the boys from the Department of Agriculture come back to prepare the land again. I am pleased that the soybeans are harvested, that I was able to nurse then along to maturity despite the scorching sun, the intermittent plagues and the problems with water. Often the pressure was too low to turn the sprinklers and I would stand, hour after hour, hose in hand, trying to get the most use from the tiny trickle spilling from the nozzle.

Sometimes my heart turns over as I look through the kitchen window and see the plants shrivelled and grotesque, the baked earth scored by a web of fine cracks like the glaze on a plate subjected to too high an oven. Then it comes to me in a flash that of course, the beans are gone, the harvest is over.

The world is uncannily quiet. I don't think anyone had any idea of how much noise even distant traffic made until we were without it. It is rare indeed for vehicles other than Government mini-cars to be seen on the streets. And there are fewer and fewer pedestrians. Those who do venture out move on their thick insulators with the slow gait of rocking-horses. Surreal and alien, they heighten rather than lessen one's sense of isolation. For one *is* isolated. We have grown used to the sight of helicopters like large dragon-flies hovering overhead – addressing us through their P.A. systems, dropping supplies – welcome but impersonal.

Dexter is my only physical contact. He is delighted to have me inside again. The heat is too great for him in the garden and as, officially, he no longer exists, we only go out under cover of dark.

The order to destroy pets, when it came, indicated more clearly than anything that had gone before, that the Government had abandoned hope. In an animal-loving culture, only direct necessity could validate such an order. It fell upon us like a heavy pall.

When the Government truck stopped by for Dexter, I reported him dead. Now that the welfare of so many depends upon our cooperation with authority, law-breaking is a serious offence. But I am not uneasy about breaking this law. As long as he remains healthy and happy, Dexter and I will share our dwindling provisions.

No need to be an ecologist or dependent on non-existent media to know all life is dying and the very atmosphere of our planet is changing radically. Already no birds sing in the hideous hot dawns as the sun, rising through a haze of dust, sheds its curious bronze-green light on a brown world. The trees that once gave us shade stand leafless now in an infernal winter. Yet as if in the masts and riggings of ships, St. Elmo's fire flickers and shines in their high branches, and bioplasmic pyrotechnics light the dying soybeans. I am reminded of how the ghostly form of a limb remains attached to the body from which it has been amputated. And I can't help thinking of all the people who don't see the colours, the practical earth-touchers with only their blunt senses to inform them. I wonder about J. and if, since we last talked, she has perhaps been able to see the colours too. But I think not. After so many years of friendship, surely I would be able to sense her, had she broken through.

Evening…? The heat has increased greatly in the last few weeks – in a quantum leap. This has resulted immediately in two things: a steady rising of the sea level throughout the world – with panic reactions and mild flooding in coastal areas; and, at last, a noticeably higher air temperature. It is causing great physical discomfort.

It was against this probability that the authorities provided us with insulator spray. Like giant cans of pressurized shaving cream. I have shut all rooms but the kitchen and by concentrating my insulating zeal on this one small area, we have managed to keep fairly cool. The word is relative, of course. The radio has stopped giving temperature readings and I have no thermometer. I have filled all cracks and crannies with the foaming plastic, even applied a layer to the exterior wall. There are no baths, of course, and no cold drinks. On the other hand I've abandoned clothes and given Dexter a shave and a haircut. Myself as well. We are a fine pair. Hairless and naked.

When the world state of emergency was declared we didn't need to be told that science had given up. The official line had been that the process would reverse itself as inexplicably as it had begun. The official policy – to hold out as long as possible. With this in mind, task forces worked day and night on survival strategy. On the municipal level, which is all I really knew about, everything that could be centralized was. Telephone exchanges, hydro plants, radio stations became centres around which vital activities took place. Research teams investigated the effects of heat on water mains, sewer pipes, electrical wiring; work crews were employed to prevent, protect or even destroy incipient causes of fire, flood and asphyxiation.

For some time now the city has been zoned. In each zone a large building has been selected, stocked with food, medical supplies and insulating materials. We have been provided with zone maps and an instruction sheet telling us to stay where we are until ordered to move to what is euphemistically called our 'home'. When ordered, we are to load our cars with whatever we still have of provisions and medicines and drive off *at once*. Helicopters have already dropped kits with enough gasoline for the trip and a small packet, somewhat surprisingly labelled 'emergency rations' which contains one cyanide capsule – grim reminder that all may not go as the planners plan. We have been asked to mark our maps, in advance, with the shortest route from our house to our 'home', so that in a crisis we will know what we are doing. These instructions are repeated *ad nauseam* over the radio, along with hearty assurances that everything is under control and that there is no cause for alarm. The Government station is now all that remains of our multi-media. When it is not broadcasting instructions, its mainly pre-recorded tapes sound inanely complacent and repetitive. Evacuation Day, as we have been told again and again, will be announced by whistle blast. Anyone who runs out of food before that or who is in need of medical aid is to use the special gas ration and go 'home' at once.

As a long-time preserver of fruits and vegetables, I hope to hold out until E. Day. When that time comes it will be a sign that broadcasts are no longer possible, that contact can no longer be maintained between the various areas of the community, that the process will not reverse itself in time and that, in fact, our world is well on the way to becoming – oh, wonder of the modern kitchen – a self-cleaning oven.

Spring, Summer, Winter, Fall. What season is it after all? I sense the hours by some inner clock. I have applied so many layers of insulating spray that almost no heat comes through from outside. But we have to have air and the small window I have left exposed acts like a furnace. Yet through it I see the dazzling colours; sense my fellow-men.

Noon. The sun is hidden directly overhead. The world is topaz. I see it through the minute eye of my window. I, the perceiving organ that peers through the house's only aperture. We are one, the house and I – parts of some vibrating sensitive organism in which Dexter plays his differentiated but integral role. The light enters us, dissolves us. We are the golden motes in the jewel.

Midnight. The sun is directly below. Beneath the burning soles of my arching feet it shines, a globe on fire. Its rays penetrate the earth. Upward beaming, they support and sustain us. We are held aloft, a perfectly balanced ball in the jet of a golden fountain. Light, dancing, infinitely upheld.

Who knows how much later. I have just 'buried' Dexter.

This morning I realized this hot little cell was no longer a possible place for a dog.

I had saved one can of dog food against this day. As I opened it Dexter's eyes swivelled in the direction of so unexpected and delicious a smell. He struggled to his feet, joyous, animated. The old Dexter. I was almost persuaded to delay, to wait and see if the heat subsided. What if tomorrow we awakened to rain? But something in me, stronger than this wavering self, carried on with its purpose.

He sat up, begging, expectant.

I slipped the meat out of the can.

'You're going to have a really good dinner,' I said, but as my voice was unsteady, I stopped.

I scooped a generous portion of the meat into his dish and placed it on the floor. He was excited, and as always when excited about food, he was curiously ceremonial, unhurried – approaching his dish and backing away from it, only to approach it again at a slightly different angle. As if the exact position was of the greatest importance. It was one of his most amusing and endearing characteristics. I let him eat his meal in his own leisurely and appreciative manner and then, as I have done so many times before, I fed him his final *bonne bouche* by hand. The cyanide pill, provided by a beneficient Government for me, went down in a gulp.

I hadn't expected it to be so sudden. Life and death so close. His small frame convulsed violently, then collapsed. Simultaneously, as if synchronized, the familiar 'shake' occurred in my vision. Dexter glowed brightly, whitely, like phosphorus. In that dazzling, light-filled moment he was no longer a small dead dog lying there. I could have thought him a lion, my sense of scale had so altered. His beautiful body blinded me with its fires.

With the second 'shake' his consciousness must have entered mine for I felt a surge in my heart as if his loyalty and love had flooded it. And like a kind of ground bass, I was aware of scents and sounds I had not known before. Then a great peace filled me – an immense space, light and sweet – and I realized that this was death. Dexter's death.

But how describe what is beyond description?

As the fires emanating from his slight frame died down, glowed weakly, residually, I put on my insulators and carried his body into the now fever-hot garden. I laid him on what had been at one time an azalea bed. I was unable to dig a grave in the baked earth or to cover him with leaves. But there are no predators now to pick the flesh from his bones. Only the heat which will, in time, desiccate it.

I returned to the house, opening the door as little as possible to prevent the barbs and briars of burning air from entering with me. I sealed the door from inside with foam sealer.

The smell of the canned dog food permeated the kitchen. It rang in my nostrils. Olfactory chimes, lingering, delicious. I was intensely aware of Dexter. Dexter immanent. I contained him as simply as a dish contains water. But the simile is not exact. For I missed his physical presence. One relies on the physical more than I had known. My hands sought palpable contact. The flesh forgets slowly.

Idly, abstractedly, I turned on the radio. I seldom do now as the batteries are low and they are my last. Also, there is little incentive. Broadcasts are intermittent and I've heard the old tapes over and over.

But the Government station was on the air. I tuned with extreme care and placed my ear close to the speaker. A voice, faint, broken by static, sounded like that of the Prime Minister.

'... all human beings can do, your Government has done for you.' (Surely not a political speech *now*?) 'But we have failed. Failed to hold back the heat. Failed to protect ourselves against it; to protect you against it. It is with profound grief that I send this farewell message to you all.' I realized that this, too, had been pre-recorded, reserved for the final broadcast. 'Even now, let us not give up hope ...'

And then, blasting through the speech, monstrously loud in the stone-silent world, the screech of the whistle summoning us 'home'. I could no longer hear the P.M.'s words.

I began automatically, obediently, to collect my few remaining foodstuffs, reaching for a can of raspberries, the last of the crop to have grown in my garden when the dawns were dewy and cool and noon sun fell upon us like golden pollen. My hand stopped in mid-air.

I would not go 'home'.

The whistle shrilled for a very long time. A curious great steam-driven cry – man's last. Weird that our final utterance should be this anguished inhuman wail.

The end. Now that it is virtually too late, I regret not having kept a daily record. Now that the part of me that writes has become nearly absorbed, I feel obliged to do the best I can.

I am down to the last of my food and water. Have lived on little for some days – weeks, perhaps. How can one measure passing time? Eternal time grows like a tree, its roots in my heart. If I lie on my back I see winds moving in its high branches and a chorus of birds is singing in its leaves. The song is sweeter than any music I have ever heard.

My kitchen is as strange as I am myself. Its walls bulge with many layers of spray. It is without geometry. Like the inside of an eccentric Styrofoam coconut. Yet, with some inner eye, I see its intricate mathematical structure. It is as ordered and no more random than an atom.

My face is unrecognizable in the mirror. Wisps of short damp hair. Enormous eyes. I swim in their irises. Could I drown in the pits of their pupils?

Through my tiny window when I raise the blind, a dead world shines. Sometimes dust storms fill the air with myriad particles burning bright and white as the lion body of Dexter. Sometimes great clouds swirl, like those from which saints receive revelations.

The colours are almost constant now. There are times when, light-headed, I dance a dizzying dance, feel part of that whirling incandescent matter – what I might once have called inorganic matter!

On still days the blameless air, bright as a glistening wing, hangs over us, hangs its extraordinary beneficence over us.

We are together now, united, indissoluble. Bonded.

Because there is no expectation, there is no frustration.

Because there is nothing we can have, there is nothing we can want.

We are hungry of course. Have cramps and weakness. But they are as if in *another body*. Our body is inviolate. Inviolable.

We share one heart.

We are one with the starry heavens and our bodies are stars.

Inner and outer are the same. A continuum. The water in the locks is level. We move to a higher water. A high sea.

A ship could pass through.

(iv)

❀ *The Selves*

Every other day I am an invalid.
Lie back among the pillows and white sheets
lackadaisical O lackadaisical.
Brush my hair out like a silver fan.
Allow myself to be wheeled into the sun.
Calves'-foot jelly, a mid-morning glass of port,
these I accept and rare azaleas in pots.

The nurses humour me. They call me 'dear'.
I am pilled and pillowed into another sphere
and there my illness rules us like a queen,
is absolute monarch, wears a giddy crown
and I, its humble servant at all times, am its least
serf on occasion and excluded from the feast.

Every other *other* day I am as fit
as planets circling.
I brush my hair into a golden sun,
strike roses from a bush,
rare plants in pots
blossom within the green of my eyes, I am
enviable O I am enviable.

Somewhere in between the two, a third
wishes to speak, cannot make itself heard,
stands unmoving, mute, invisible,
a bolt of lightning in its naked hand.

❈ *The Filled Pen*

Eager to draw again,
find space in that small room
for my drawing-board and inks
and the huge revolving world
the delicate nib releases.

I have only to fill my pen
and the shifting gears begin:
flywheel and cogwheel start
their small-toothed interlock

and whatever machinery draws
is drawing through my fingers
and the shapes that I have drawn
gaze up into my eyes.
We stare each other down.

Light of late afternoon –
white wine across my paper –
the subject I would draw.
Light of the stars and sun.

Light of the swan-white moon.
The blazing light of trees.
And the rarely glimpsed bright face
behind the apparency of things.

❀ *Snowshoes*

Flat   twin
lacrosse sticks
laced
with oil-lamp wicks

Two eyes
of Horus
one above the other

I smell wet moccasins
see beads on fire

What a beautiful lattice:
babiche: pale strips
of wolf gut
stretched
on wooden frames
Red bobbles
on far toe-tips

It is twenty below

The air burning

Fingers are thick and slow
Lumps of lead
at the ends of my legs
move rattan pontoons
through a smoke of snow

I climb a drift
hear it pack
and hold
sky-high on the prairie

This engineering –
the reverse of wings –
is achieved from below

How is it on water?

The question
never
quite beyond earshot
comes wagging   comes wagging

❀ *After Reading* Albino Pheasants *by Patrick Lane*

Pale beak ... pale eye ... the dark imagination
flares like magnesium. Add but *pale flesh*
and I am lifted to a weightless world:
watered cerulean, chrome-yellow (light)
and green, veronese – if I remember – a soft wash
recalls a summer evening sky.

At Barra de Navidad we watched the sky
fade softly like a bruise. Was it imagination
that showed us Venus phosphorescent in a wash
of air and ozone? – a phosphorescence flesh
wears like a mantle in bright moonlight,
a natural skin-tone in that other world.

Why should I wish to escape this world?
Why should three phrases alter the colour of the sky
the clarity, texture even, of the light?
What is there about the irrepressible imagination
that the adjective *pale* modifying *beak, eye* and *flesh*
can set my sensibilities awash?

If with my thickest brush I were to lay a wash
of thinnest watercolour I could make a world
as unlike my own dense flesh
as the high-noon midsummer sky;
but it would not catch at my imagination
or change the waves or particles of light

yet *pale* can tip the scales, make light
this heavy planet. If I were to wash
everything I own in mercury, would imagination
run rampant in that suddenly silver world –
free me from gravity, set me floating sky-
ward – thistledown – permanently disburdened of my flesh?

Like cygnets hatched by ducks, our minds and flesh
are imprinted early – what to me is light
may be dark to one born under a sunny sky.
And however cool the water my truth won't wash
without shrinking except in its own world
which is one part matter, nine parts imagination.

I fear flesh which blocks imagination,
the light of reason which constricts the world.
Pale beak ... pale eye ... pale flesh ... My sky's awash.

❀ The Maze

I clearly recall the feel of the clipped hedges –
laurel or box – I am not sure which.
I was still small
so the little leaves of box
would have seemed bigger.
I remember they shone, looked black in places, scratched
the skin of my wrists and ankles as I passed.

Overhead the sky was light,
a faint cirrus,
duck-egg changing to golden like a wing,
but the shadow cast by the hedge
threw a chill upon me
as I kept to the curve that drew me in
and in.
Compelled, and carrying out a strange instruction –
vital, timeless, tangible as a thread –
I was tracing the spiral nebula in my head.

When I think of it now I remember the path frozen
and how, on the inside edge of a bowed skate,
I arrived at the heart of the maze in a clean sweep,
reached 'le Ciel' in a long unbroken spiral.

Yet the truth of the matter escapes.
There is no returning
beyond the sudden narrowing of the curve –
(eye of the nautilus, the ram's horn).
Memory fails me at every try.
I follow
the spiralling pathway over and over, run –
hoping to pass that place on the sharpening turn –
to grow small, then smaller, smaller still – and enter
the maze's vanishing point, a spark, extinguished.

Great desire to write it all.
Is it age, death's heavy breath
making absolute autobiography
urgent?

Who would think that this old hive
housed such honey?
Could one guess
blue and gold of a macaw
blue and gold of sky and sun
could set up such melodic din
beat so musical a drum?

Distilled from all this living,
all this gold.

1. To begin before I was born.
   Little Joy riding a cloud
   saw it all, merely smiled –
   this planet's snares, seducers, tears –
   knew it all. Simply smiled.

2. Man in black.
   Raggedy jacket, shiny pants.
   Victim of St Vitus' dance.
   Animated scarecrow made of bones,
   jerking, tweaking down the street.
   Strings tangled.
   Nerves jangled.
           My small pink coat
           my scarlet shoes
           drained of colour,
           somehow ... broke.

3. They removed her golden wig.
   Underneath, as if trepanned,
   her head was like a china cup.
   Eyes that could no longer shut
   were taken out.
   Realigned, the leaden weight.
   Glassy eyes in pairs on hooks
   stared in dozens from the walls.
      That visit finished me for dolls.

4. A woman with wet palms who took my hand.
      I prayed the Lord my palms be wet.

5. Lost ring. Lost ring.
   She lost it. Lost it.
   Pain
   of that loss
   lay on us
   summerlong.
   And then to my bright eye
   the gleam in the grass.
   The gold in the green
   beneath the snow-apple tree.
      I glimpsed the changed
      geometry of Eden.
      Transparent bird
      in its transparent shell.

6. White quartz
   red-veined,
   cerulean-veined
   and jade,
   found in the crawl-space
   under the veranda
   with grown-ups walking
   talking overhead.
      My secret garden.
      Magic. Mineral.

7. Horse. High as a house. Smooth as a nut.
   Its flaring nostrils snorted dragon's breath
   or snuffled, tickling. Its velvet lips
   lifted the accurate white sugar lump
   exactly from my flat extended palm.
   And crunch. The curving yellowish ivory teeth.

8. Agates and alleys. Smokies. Glassies.
   Tumbling galaxies of them. Worlds.
   A dark disappearing one that whirled
   and a spiral one that drew me in
   to vanishing point at its poles.

9. Backdrop: the cordillera of the Rockies.
   Infinity – slowly spinning in the air –
   invisibly entered through the holes of gophers,
   visibly, in a wigwam's amethyst smoke.

   Eternity implicit on the prairie.
   One's self the centre of a boundless dome
   so balanced in its horizontal plane
   and sensitively tuned that one's least move
   could fractionally tip it North, South, East.

   Westward, in undulations of beige turf,
   the fugal foothills changed their rhythm, rose
   to break in fire and snow. My Hindu Kush.
           It was a landscape in which things could grow
           enormous. Full of struts. A prairie sky
           builds an immense Meccano
           piling high
           shapes its horizon levels.

10. In blizzards, blurred small Indian cayuses
    drifted like icebergs, furred, a dirty white.
    Browsed among wild crocuses. Stampeded
    like weathered black machines,
    their pistons shaking
    tiger lily, dog rose.

11. Unlighted fireworks –
    the bright Sarcees
    slumbered among us in a dream.
    Chiefs in their eagle-feather haloes –
    intricate beadwork, quillwork,
    (stipple, stroke).
    Upright papooses, portable in quivers,
    black-eyed as saskatoons.

12. Wind whipping us, rain pricking,
    poplars bending.
    Through a stream of all my hair,
    gleam of my father's spurs,
    our jingling bridles,
    the grave-box, lidless, open
    where we rode:
    string figure in bangles and rags.
    Small corpse picked to the bone.
            Dusk fell.
            In all my cells dusk fell.
            My shroud or winding sheet.
            O bind me
            tight against this eye
            this prairie eye
            that stares and stares.
            O hide me safe
            in cleft or coulee
            fold me
            in leaves or blowing
            grasses.
            Hold me.
            Hold me.

❀ *Full Moon*

I search all cupboards for my lunar topee
and find its crescent-shaped
bull's horns
glimmering phosphorus among my hats –
a Minotaur among domestic sheep.

Pale female Viking venturing into night,
I dare the full moon's innocent vague stare
in Mother Goddess guise
while left and right
my sober neighbours beat their wives and rave.

❀ Dwelling Place

This habitation – bones and flesh and skin –
where I reside, proceeds through sun and rain
a mobile home with windows and a door
and pistons plunging, like a soft machine.

Conforming as a bus, its 'metal' is
more sensitive than chrome or brass. It knows
a pebble in its shoe or heat or cold.
I scrutinize it through some aperture

that gives me godsview – see it twist and change.
It sleeps, it weeps, its poor heart breaks,
it dances like a bear, it laughs, opines
(and therefore *is*). It has a leafy smell

of being young in all the halls of heaven.
It serves a term in anterooms of hell,
greying and losing lustre. It is dull.
A lifeless empty skin. I plot its course

and watch it as it moves – a house, a bus;
I, its inhabitant, indweller – eye
to that tiny chink where two worlds meet –
or – if you so discern it – two divide.

❀ *Difficult*

You would lead me into a world where I may not go.
I am trying to climb the Royal Tree. Its trunk
is slippery elm. A tiny crown
its intricate branches high above my head.

Difficult. It is difficult until I grow
little thorns on soles and palms
and cat's-tongue patches on my arms and thighs.
I see you from the corner of my eye

and it is difficult, seeing you. You are
beckoning. You are as beautiful as
fairy tales. You are the prince
stepped from the shape of the beast.

It is difficult to look away, to think
only of tree – no branch in sight,
the smooth trunk slippery as ice, the height
frightening.

It is the Royal Tree. Up here it has
no shape or colour. I can see
a segment only of its trunk
trunktrunktrunktrunktrunktrunktrunktrunk.

And sky. Why am I
in this precarious place? Sky has hypnotic powers, I
hear voices. Bird notes
contain messages. Even the wind

speaks of your features as if you were God
GodGodGodGod. Words repeat and repeat.
I do not understand quite simple sentences.
Soon they will put me away.

❀ The Tethers

You are my tethers – you and you and you:
beautiful, ailing, witty or beloved.
You hold my tent-pole upright
make my tent
symmetrical and true –
you guy-ropes of a tent
that would not be a tent.

Think what a sail I'd make
against the blue –
flying! – for God's sake.
What a splendid din
the whip and rattle of my canvas wings
flapping me upward
ragged as a crane.

Not as I dreamed:
tent formless, beyond form.
But as I never dreamed:
tent shapeless, without shape.

(v)

✤ The Disguises

You, my Lord, were dressed in astonishing disguises:
as a Chinese emperor, ten feet tall,
as a milk-skinned woman
parading in exquisite stuffs.

You were ambiguous and secret
and hidden in other faces.

How did we know you were there at all?
Your ineffable presence
perfumed the air like an avenue of lilacs.

✤ After Donne

A door whines and I go. Or a fly drones
and reactive, I almost buzz.
Am subject to every tic and toc.
Ears' energy frenetic.
Likewise eyes'.
Distractable.
Unexpected red, green, blue
signal and I respond.

For the least moving speck
I neglect God and all his angels,
yet attention's funnel –
a macaw's eye – contracts,
becomes a vortex.

I have been sucked through.

❈ Song ... Much of It Borrowed

How beautifully it sings.
How beautifully Sitwell sang it.
How beautifully Donne began it:
'that God is an angel in an angel
and a stone in a stone
and a straw in a straw'.

I knew it all before
but *The Canticle of the Rose*
a long time on my shelf
and hidden by some flaw –
a kind of shelf in myself –
was suddenly visible

and that golden rain of poems
that glorious storm of poems
sang until they were heard:
that God is a poet in a poet
a poem in a poem
and a word in a word.

❈ Star-Gazer

The very stars are justified.
The galaxy
italicized.

I have proofread
and proofread
the beautiful script.

There are no
errors.

❀ *Chinese Boxes*

Box within box.
I know the order, know
large to small diminishing until
that cube the size of sugar – like a die –
is cast within its core
and therein set – dimensionless –
an all-ways turning eye –
a dot, an aleph, which
with one swift glance
sees heaven and hell united
as a globe
in whose harmonious spinning
day and night
and birth and death are conjured into one,
where seasons lie like compass points
and where, twinned with its answers,
question is born null.

Box within box.
From small to large increasing –
angles, blocks,
enormous, made of plexiglas,
the sky
filling with them,
visible as air
is visible when briefly smoked with breath
until their structures grow too large and sheer
for sight to encompass –
cellophane box kites
huge as the Kaaba
luminous as ice
and imperceptible to any sense
more coarse than sightings of that inner eye
which sees the absolute
in emptiness.

❄ *At Sea*

True devotion is for itself: not
to desire heaven nor to fear hell.

RABIA EL-ADEWIA, 8th c.

Rounding the salt-rimed deck
riding the tilting sea
sky grey
seabirds wheeling,
head down in despair,
in treadmill trapped,
in thoughts
revolving, churning, churning;
a stranger from a chair,
(one I had passed before
how many times unseeing?)
rose – and as if her words
were butterfly or bird
lighting upon my wrist,
blue butterfly of Brazil,
hoopoe perhaps or rare
landbird from who-knows-where,
weightless upon my wrist,
trembling brilliant there –
stopped the machine and brought
its grinding to a halt.

and in that silence spoke

I don't know what she said
only that my despair
vanished and standing there
sky grey
seabirds wheeling
I knew as I looked at her
tweed coat and blowing hair
that she was Rabia.

❀ Spinning

Hurl your giant thunderbolt that on my heart
falls gently as a feather, falls and fills
each crease and cranny of me – a chinook:
sweet water, head to foot.

With lightning stagger me so I may stand
centred as never otherwise. In stock-
stillness, dizzying movement find.
Spinning, a dot.

All-of-a-piece, seamless; with the warp and woof
afterwards/before. The stuff spun
without stop or selvedge – measureless
continuum.

Visible/invisible. Golden. Clear
as any crystal. How to name it? How
to loose or hold – for held is holder here
and holder held.

Harry me. Hurry me to spaces where
my Father's house has many dimensions.
Tissue of tesseract.
A sphered sphere.

❁ *Three Gold Fish*

I feel quite sure those three gold fish I saw
burning like Blake's *Tyger* in the pool
were real all right.
The pool was different too.
It seemed to swell
like some great crystalline and prismed tear
and brim and never spill
and those fish burned within it
burned and shone
and left their brand –
a piscine fleur-de-lys –
stamped on the air, on me,
on skin and hair
spinning to giddy heaven.

Sharp and clear
that fiery image burns within me still:
those three gold fish
the pool
the altered air
and I – observing and observed –
a high
point on a twirling spindle which
spun and hurled great gilded lariats.

❧ The Yellow People in Metamorphosis

Lunar Phase
Not only silvered
One dimension less

Moon's light
falls thin and flat

on metal shapes
that heave and strive

immobile
but alive

Earthly Phase
1. In topazes and amber
   mango, peach
   the yellow people hive
   the yellow people swarm
   just beyond our hearing
   just beyond our sight
   Their chromosomes
   and yellow genes
   squeezed from a tube
   of cadmium
   their canary-coloured
   hair and skin
   and eyes
   are palest
   cadmium

   Molecular
   they stretch and grow
   Don waggish wigs
   wear caps, capes, cloaks
   gamboge and chrome
   Crave mosaics

small Moorish patterns
checks   Greek key
all intricate shapes
fine mottle   stipple
singing reeds
whistles of birds

Whose notes are these?
That trill? Did (s)he
flicker a yellow throat muscle?
Do wiry yellow curls vibrate?
A springed instrument? Is s(he)
crossed with a flute?
That crown
a splendid yellow bony comb
grown from the cranium

The yellow people hive
the yellow people swarm
just beyond our hearing
just beyond belief

Warblers in the leaves?
Peaches in the trees?
An antic
trick
of light?

2. Stamp   Stamp   I feel them weighty
   Wonderful acrobats clanking about
   loud in the next dimension
   luring my inner eye
   and growing huge and yellow
   Ballooning gunny-sacks
   striving to sunhood
   not yet sunny
   rayed
   as dandelions
   and lighter far

than their looming size suggests
See them throw ballast up to another ether
Ascend
hand over fist

Yet one least glance aside
shows me their scale of gold
ladders that come and go
They alter as they climb
and shining chains and cones
reach down to draw them up
as   known to unknown spanned
with weightless veins and bones
transforming all their yellow
they golden   glow
and
        vanish

3. An orison of them stars my farthest heaven

Vertical
these almost alchemists
gilders of nimbi
leaf the chieftain's feathers
Sol's flames   cock's crest
bright Leo's sunburst locks

Make sovereign all my pocketful of copper

   Solar Phase
This is another matter
Seventh heaven
Among celestial celandines to eat
one apple for eternity

(I know
nothing of what I speak
I speak
nothing of what I know)

❀ About the Author

P.K. Page was born in England and brought up on the Canadian prairies. She was out of the country for many years with her diplomat-husband, Arthur Irwin, and now lives in Victoria, British Columbia. She is the author of more than a dozen books of poetry, fiction, and non-fiction, including three books for children. Among other honours, she has won the Governor General's Award for poetry. She is a visual artist whose works are represented in the National Gallery of Canada and the Art Gallery of Ontario and in other distinguished collections. The Winter 1996 number of *The Malahat Review* is a tribute to her life and work.